MARY
Queen of the Palace
Mistress of the House

EDWARD HALLINAN

Parresia Books 2009

CHANDLER
BOOK DESIGN

First published in Great Britain
by Parresia Books 2009.

Parresia Books
113 Whinney Lane, New Ollerton,
Newark, NG22 9TJ.
www.parresia-books.co.uk

ISBN 978-0-9561860-0-3

Cover Photo: ©istockphoto.com/Hazlan Abdul Hakim

Cover designed and typeset in Palatino 10pt by
Chandler Book Design, King's Lynn, Norfolk
www.chandlerbookdesign.co.uk

Printed and bound by
MPG Books Group in the UK

For my wife Elizabeth

To Lesley,

With fond memories and respect for your wisdom.

Ed.

(Edward Mallinson)

31st May 2010

ACKNOWLEDGEMENTS

rofound gratitude to my step-daughter Natalya Garzon and to Al Brown for all their skill, efforts and hard work on successive versions of the manuscript of this book. Thanks also to the staff at Maltby and New Ollerton libraries for their unfailing courtesy and patience in searching for, ordering and obtaining books. To my sister, Alison Yiangou, for the gift of membership to the London Library, as well as for books, all of which were invaluable.

Also to Alison for introducing me to the Beshara School of Intensive Esoteric Education, which runs courses established by Bulent Rauf (1911–1987) which involve study, meditation and other spiritual practices and disciplines, and work. The study is mainly centred upon the works of Muhyiddin Ibn 'Arabi (1165–1240), known as the Sheikh Al-Aqbar (the greatest master). His works contain without a doubt the most concise, complete and explicit exposition of the Unity of Being from the standpoint of Universality ever committed to writing.

It was whilst attending these courses that I met Bulent Rauf and Dom Sylvester Houédard OSB (1925–1992).[1] Bulent Rauf is a spiritual heir of Muhyiddin Ibn 'Arabi. Bulent's life was a demonstration of the Unity of

Being and the Universality of the essence of the works of Muhyiddin Ibn 'Arabi, and who is, accordingly, a living demonstration of the principle of making Mary our mother too. Dom Sylvester Houédard, Benedictine monk of Prinknash Abbey, was a man of such monumental learning that, on one occasion when he was walking by, Dr Ralph Austin (formerly lecturer in Arabic in the University of Durham, and an authority on Islamic mysticism) remarked with profound respect 'There goes the whole of medieval Christendom'. Profound learning which was combined, as with Bulent Rauf, with an equally profound humility. Whenever he spoke or whatever he wrote, he would move from St Benedict, to Muhyiddin Ibn 'Arabi; from the Cappadocians to Meister Eckhart; from St Augustine to St Thomas Aquinas; from Philo to the Buddhist Masters 'without effort and as if naturally' (as in the twelfth degree of humility of St Benedict) because for him there was no difference. Thus Dom Sylvester once gave a seminar on a sermon of Meister Eckhart filled with references to Muhyiddin Ibn 'Arabi and illustrated by a Buddhist icon.

On a visit to the tomb of Mevlana Jalalu'l-din Rumi at Konya in Turkey, someone once said to Bulent, 'You must love Rumi very much to come every year', to which Bulent replied 'No'. The person was astonished, whereupon Bulent said 'We love what Rumi loves and what Rumi loves, loves Rumi'. Bulent and Dom Sylvester both love what Muhyiddin Ibn 'Arabi loves and what Muhyiddin Ibn 'Arabi loves, loves Muhyiddin Ibn 'Arabi, loves Bulent Rauf, loves Dom Sylvester. Accordingly, both Bulent and Dom Sylvester are, in the very highest sense and meaning of the expression, Men of God. Muhyiddin Ibn 'Arabi wrote:

> Oh marvel! A garden amidst fires! My heart has become capable of every form: it is a Pasture for gazelles and a convent for Christian monks, And

a temple for idols and the pilgrim's *Ka'ba* and the
Tables of the Torah and the book of the *Qur'an*. I
follow the religion of Love: whatever way Love's
Camels take, that is my religion and my faith.[2]

Bulent and Dom Sylvester, two men who knew indeed
the marvel of a garden amidst fires, whose hearts truly
were capable of every form and truly were a pasture for
gazelles and a convent for Christian monks, a temple for
idols and the pilgrim's *Ka'ba* and the Tables of the Torah
and the book of the *Qur'an*; who truly did follow the
religion of Love; whose religion and faith truly did indeed
consist in following Love's camels whatever way they take
and who are, accordingly, in the very highest sense and
meaning, friends of God and, therefore, God's friends. So I
would like to thank Alison and her husband Peter and all
the Trustees of the Beshara Trust and all the Directors of
the Chisholme Institute over the twenty-seven years since
I first attended courses.

It is also only fitting to acknowledge the spiritual
influences which have shaped whatever is proper in this
work and without which it could not have been written;
all of whom are representatives of Universality at Its very
highest level:

Ismail Hakki Bursevi (1653–1725), Mevlana Jalalu'l-din
Rumi (1207–73), Saint Benedict (c. 480–550), the four great
Cappadocian Fathers: Saint Basil the Great (c. 329/330–1st
January 379), his younger brother, Saint Gregory of Nyssa
(c. 330–395), their friend, Saint Gregory Nazianzos (c.
328/9-389/90) and Saint Amphilochios (c. 340–395). Saint
Amphilochios was Bishop of Iconium, the modern Konya
in Turkey, from 373. He was the first cousin of Saint Gregory
Nazianzos and the spiritual son of Saint Basil the Great. The
Cappadocians and their antecedents: Philo of Alexandria
(c. 25/20 BCE–ACE50/51), whose influence on the whole
of mysticism was profound, Origen (c. 185–254), Saint

Gregory Thaumaturgos (c.213–270) and their successors, most notably Evagrios of Pontos (c. 345/6–399) and Saint Maximos Confessor (c. 580–662). Finally, but by no means leastly, Meister Eckhart (c. 1260–1328).

In addition, Joseph Campbell (1904-1987), René Guénon (1886–1951), Titus Burckhardt (1908–1984), Heinrich Zimmer (1890–1943), Marija Gimbutas (1921–1994), Gertrude Rachel Levy (1884–1966) and Karl Kerényi (1897–1973).

It should also be acknowledged that whatever is improper in this work is entirely due to the ignorance and lack of tact of the author, for which he begs forgiveness of God, of Mary and of the Saints. For whatever is proper, appropriate and, above all, tactful, the praise and the thanks are to God and then thanks are due to Mary and the Saints.

Notes

1. Unless otherwise stated, all references to the sayings of Dom Sylvester are taken from the author's memories of times spent with him, whether at Seminars or in conversations with him.

2. *The Tarjumán Al-Ashwáq. A Collection of Mystical Odes by Muhyiddin Ibn 'Arabi*, trans. by Reynold A. Nicholson, (London: Theosophical Publishing House Ltd, 1978 repr.), p. 67.

CONTENTS

INTRODUCTION

ary: *Queen of the Palace, Mistress of the House* is an exploration of the spiritual meaning of seven from amongst the series of mosaics of the life of Mary in the church of Saint Saviour in Chora (Kariye Camii) in Istanbul. The seven mosaics are:

1. The Birth of Mary.
2. The First Seven Steps of Mary.
3. The Presentation of Mary into the Temple.
4. The Annunciation.
5. The Nativity.
6. The Crucifixion.
7. The Koimesis (the Dormition, or Assumption, of Mary).

The purpose of this exploration is to show how each one of these mosaics in its own right, as well as the seven together, is and are a demonstration of our meaning and purpose, our spiritual meaning and purpose, as being created according to the 'image' and the 'likeness' of God, and that the Principle of Mary, the Meaning of Mary, plays an essential role both in our original creation and in our being able to realise and fulfil that meaning within ourselves.

For Saint Basil the Great 'that which the Word communicates by sound, the painting shows forth silently by representation'. Which words were echoed by the Fathers of the Seventh (and last) Ecumenical Council, the Second Council of Nicaea (787), 'through these two mediums which accompany each other...we acquire knowledge of the same realities'.[1]

The Word, the *Logos*, is God's Knowledge of Himself as He Himself is and God is His Knowledge of Himself. Everything in creation is a 'word' of God, and the eternal words, the *logoi*, the *ayan-i-thabita* of Islamic spirituality, which are the eternal essences or principles both of ourselves and of the whole of creation, are contained in eternity within the Word, the *Logos*. Within Christian spirituality, God the Father is the First Person of the Holy Trinity and the Word, the *Logos*, is the Second Person.

Saint John says that 'God is Love' (I John 4.8), and the Love which God is, *Agape* in Greek, is selfless Love, which is the giving of self. As Love, in Love, God gives Himself to Himself as He Himself is, and this Self-Gift is the Third Person of the Holy Trinity, The Holy Spirit. Through Self-Gift, the *logoi*, hidden within the *Logos* in a state of non-individuation, of non-manifestation, as colours are hidden within light, or sounds in the breath, are individuated; that is, they are manifested as individual *logoi*, and the unfoldments of that which lies within each *logos* are actualised as becomings in time. As becomings not as beings, because Being belongs to God alone, which means that being is loaned to us, and to the whole of creation, as a gift, because we, and the whole of creation, exist by way of, and only by way of, God's Self-Gift of Himself to Himself as Himself. What appears in time is not the *logoi* themselves, which remain eternal essences, but the unfoldment of that which lies within each individual *logos*.

God gives Himself to Himself as He Himself is, or one can equally well say, God speaks Himself to Himself as His own Word, and that which is given, is spoken, is God's own perfect 'image' of Himself as He Himself is within Himself, as He always and forever is within Himself, which is unaffected by Self-Gift. This is the 'image' of God according to which and after which we have all been fashioned and created. So the *Logos* is both the Eternal Word, which is God's Knowledge of Himself as He Himself is, which Knowledge God Himself is, and, by way of Self-Gift, is also the 'image'. Which is why Saint Basil the Great and the Fathers of the Christian church afforded the icon equal status with the Gospels, for the *Logos* reveals the 'image' and the 'image' reveals the *Logos*, which means that the *Logos* and the 'image', the Gospels and the icon, correspond to and complement one another.

The book of Genesis affirms that it is only we as human becomings who are created according to the 'image' and the 'likeness' of God. God's Self-Gift is God's Self-Gift of the whole of Himself to Himself, whole and entire, and in giving Himself to Himself, God gives the whole of Himself to each of the *logoi*, the eternal essences hidden within the *Logos*; but that Gift is received by each of the *logoi* according to its capacity to receive, and its capacity to receive is determined only by itself, by, that is, what it itself is. Thus, whilst it receives the whole Gift, and the whole is hidden within it, it expresses that Gift as itself, as a cat, or a stone, or a tree, for example. It is only the human becoming, who is created according to the 'image' and the 'likeness' of God, who therefore has the capacity to express and return the Gift as It is given, whole and entire: to be, that is, the perfect 'image' and 'likeness' of God, but only by way of Self-Gift. This is the 'First Birth', the birth of God into the soul.

In *Agape*, the love which God is, there is no compulsion, *Agape* is free and freely given and is given unconditionally.

Accordingly, the Gift of Love bestows upon us free will, which, in its turn, means that we are free to recognise and affirm that we exist only by way of Self-Gift, that Being belongs to God alone and is loaned to us as becomings actualised by Self-Gift, and that God is the actuality and, therefore, the Truth, both of ourselves and of the whole of creation. Thus, by abandoning the affirmation of ourselves, we allow God to appear in us and to act in us as Himself in us as His own perfect 'image' and 'likeness.' This is the Second Birth, the birth of the soul back into God.

We are equally free to deny the condition of our original creation, to deny that God is the actuality and, therefore, the Truth, both of ourselves and of the whole of creation, and to claim being for ourselves, thereby asserting ourselves as beings (rather than as becomings) beside God. Thus we create a veil, the veil of self, which Saint Benedict calls the '*obex*', between God and ourselves as He Himself is. Thus, whilst we retain the 'image', which can never be effaced, we lose the 'likeness', since in affirming ourselves rather than God, we determine over God by compelling Him to appear and to act in us as ourselves in us as His own 'image' only.

It is a fundamental principle of mysticism that at the heart of all religions and of the myths and legends of all peoples lies a universal spirituality which, whilst it reveals itself in all religions, myths and legends, is also beyond all form and forms. Myth here being used in its true and proper sense, as parable containing, hiding and revealing profound spiritual principles.

It is also a fundamental principle of spirituality that if we are alive to ourselves, that is, if we affirm ourselves by claiming being for ourselves, then we are dead to God. Dead, that is, in the sense that by so doing we have lost 'the likeness' which means that we are dead to God as He Himself is, and, conversely, we are alive to God only in as much as He accordingly manifests Himself in us as ourselves in His own 'image' only. In order to be alive to God, we must die to ourselves, as the Prophet Mohammad says, 'die before you die'. St Gregory Nazianzos says:

> Let us give ourselves entire, that we may receive back ourselves entire; for this is to receive entirely, when we give ourselves to God and offer as a sacrifice our own salvation.[2]

By 'dying' before we 'die', by giving 'ourselves entire' we submit completely to God; this is the *'potentia obedientiaris'* of St Benedict and is the meaning of Islam. This results in our being the place of sheer receptivity, pure un-conditioning receptivity whereby, and whereby alone, God's Self Gift can be received as it is given, whole and entire. Thus by 'sacrificing' ourselves, we receive back ourselves, but ourselves entire as according to the condition of our original creation, for 'the likeness' has been restored to 'the image'. It is affirmed in all religions that unless we enter into complete submission to God, it is impossible for us to return to the condition of our original creation, for 'the likeness' to be restored to 'the image'. Mary, the Principle of Mary, the Meaning of Mary, is a sublime expression for all times and all places of complete submission to God, and therefore, of unconditioning passive receptivity.

This principle is both manifested in and receives the movement of Self Gift which is the Holy Spirit; the movement which is Love and the Gift which is Beauty, and which is the First Birth, the birth of God into the soul. This is the First Grace of Christian spirituality; Grace being the movement of Self Gift, the Holy Spirit, just as the Second Birth, the birth of the soul back into God is known as Second Grace, Salvific Grace, which is the 'Deifying Light' of St Benedict. Second Grace, given to us as manifested in this world, is therefore ultimately the same as First Grace. The Second Birth can only take place as a result of the combination of our effort, the principle of Mary and Grace. Our effort, because we have to want it, so in that sense sheer receptivity, passivity, in us is an action because it does not mean that we do nothing, as Dom Sylvester never tired of saying. God wants it for us, God wishes it for us, as St Gregory Nazianzos says:

> Oh, swiftness of His mercy: oh easiness of the Covenant: this blessing may be bought by you merely for willing it; He accepts the very desire as a great price; He thirsts to be thirsted for; He gives to drink to all who desire to drink; He takes it as a kindness to be asked for the kindness; He is ready and liberal; He gives with more pleasure than others receive. Only let us not be condemned for frivolity by asking for little, and for what is unworthy of the Giver.[3]

But no matter how much God wants it for us, no matter how much 'He thirsts to be thirsted for' because His gift is given as and in Love, and because Love is freely given and without compulsion, we have to want it, to wish it, to thirst for it too. Which wanting, which wishing, which thirsting, which effort is an integral part of our submission, of, that is, the Principle of Mary, the Meaning of Mary.

It is this principle, this meaning, which has been manifested in the Goddess, the Goddess who is one, but whose names are many; the Goddess who was called Inanna by the Sumerians, Ishtar by the Babylonians, Cybele by the Phrygians, Isis, Nephthys and Hathor by the Egyptians, Aphrodite, Artemis and Hera by the Greeks, and who is called Kali in India; the same Goddess, the same Principle: the Principle of Mary, the Meaning of Mary. The Goddess in all her manifestations, under all the names by which she has been known, is no other than Mary. The Principle of

Mary, the Meaning of Mary, is manifested in the Goddess and the Goddess reaches her most profound and sublime expression in Mary.

Notes

1 Both quoted (with references to the source) in Leonid Ouspensky, *Theology of the Icon*, 2 vols (Crestwood, NY 10707-1699: St Vladimir's Seminary Press, 1992), I, p.8.

2 Nicene and Post-Nicene Fathers of the Christian Church, second series, volume VII, *Saint Cyril of Jerusalem and Saint Gregory Nazianzen*. Under the Editorial Supervision of Philip Schaff and Henry Wace, Trans. by Charles Gordon Browne, M.A., and James Swallow, M.A. (Edinburgh: T&T Clark; Grand Rapids, Michigan: WM. B. Eerdmans Publishing Company, 2nd Series Repr. 1989), Oration 40, Holy Baptism, XL, p.375.

3 Ibid. XXVII, p.370.

THE BIRTH OF MARY

s the Gospels are silent upon the life of Mary, the iconography of her life is based on two apocryphal gospels, the *Protevangelium Jacobi* and the *Gospel of Pseudo-Matthew.*

Saint Anna was sterile. She prayed under a linden tree. At the end of her prayer, an Angel appeared and announced the birth of Mary to her. Her husband, Saint Joachim, in shame at having his offerings in the temple rejected because he was childless, had fled, with his flocks, either into the desert or to a hillside. Saint Anna had not seen him for five months and did not know whether he was dead or alive. The annunciation, and the words spoken by the Angel in the annunciation of the birth of Mary to Saint Anna and Saint Joachim, reflect and prefigure the Annunciation of the birth of Christ to Mary. The *Protevangelium* tells us that the Angel said to Saint Anna 'Anna, Anna, the Lord hath heard thy prayer, and thou shalt conceive; and thy seed shall be spoken of in all the world'. In *Pseudo-Matthew*, the Angel says to Saint Anna 'Be not afraid, Anna, for there is seed for thee in the decree of God; and all generations even to the end shall wonder at that which shall be born of thee'.

In announcing the birth of Mary to Saint Joachim, the Angel says of Mary:

> She will be in the temple of God, and the Holy
> Spirit shall abide in her; and her blessedness shall
> be greater than that of all the holy women, so that
> no one can say that any before her has been like
> her, or that any after her in this world will be so.
>
> And of Saint Anna, the angel says 'and her
> seed shall be blessed, and she herself shall be
> blessed, and shall be made the mother of eternal
> blessing'.[1]

In the mosaic of the birth of Mary, St Anna is sitting up on a bed, looking at Mary, who is about to be bathed by a midwife, whilst a maid fills the bath. Another maid is preparing the crib. Four young women, bearing gifts, are approaching the bed. Behind them, another young woman is holding a fan made of peacock feathers. St Joachim is shown standing in a doorway, his head bowed, his right arm across his chest, looking in. A scarlet veil stretches across the background architecture.

The scene of the bathing is included in all icons of the birth of Mary, as the bathing of the newly born Christ child is included in all icons of the Nativity, as the bathing of the newly born Saint forms part of the icons of all Saints where the icon includes scenes from the life of the Saint around the borders. This is not a charming, naturalistic detail; on the contrary, it is a demonstration of a profound spiritual meaning. The Prophet Mohammad said that he had been born in the normal way because people said that because the birth of Christ was special and unlike their birth, it was, accordingly, impossible for them to realise within themselves the meaning of Christ because they had not been born in the same way. That is, they failed to realise the spiritual meaning of the birth of Christ. The Prophet also said to his followers 'I am a man like all of you', and this is why the scene of the bathing of the newly born Christ child, the newly born Mary, the newly born Saint is included. It is saying to us that this is possible for us too. This is the purpose of every icon, of every sacred text: to say that it is possible for each and every one of us to realise and fulfil the meaning of our original creation by returning, by way of the Second Birth, to that condition as according to both 'the image' and 'the likeness' of God.

Water, in this world, is the 'lower waters', the 'waters below' of Genesis and is a symbol of, and therefore, a revelation of, the 'upper waters', the 'waters above', the Primeval Ocean. The Primeval Ocean, which is both manifested in and receives the movement of Self-Gift, is Prime Matter, whose interior is the Holy Spirit. Prime Matter is sheer receptivity, which is the Principle and Meaning of Mary, by means of which, together with the Holy Spirit, both births take place within the soul. This is why water, which is essentially shapeless and colourless, has the capacity to assume all colours and all shapes whilst yet remaining essentially shapeless and colourless; which is itself a sign that God Who in Himself is above and beyond all form manifests and reveals Himself by way of form, whose actuality He is.

It is by way of the Principle and Meaning of Mary, that, by way of Self-Gift, we are cleansed of, purified of, that separate self, since it is washed away from us. Accordingly, in this world, water possesses purifying and cleansing properties, and travelling across water represents an ablution, a purification, a return from the waters below to the waters above. A return, that is, to the Principle and the Meaning of Mary, whereby, by way of Self-Gift, the soul is born back into God.

In the Holy *Qur'an*, God says 'from water we brought forth all living things'. That human life begins in water, in the amniotic fluid of the womb, and that all life on earth began in water, in the ocean, are signs that all individuated life began in eternity with the reception of the Gift in the upper waters, which were themselves manifested in the Gift. And this process manifests itself in this world by way of human life beginning in water, in the amniotic fluid of the womb, and all life on earth beginning in water, in the ocean.

The bath being filled is circular in shape and rests upon a stand—that is, it has the same shape as a chalice. It is the empty vessel (as is also the vessel with which the maiden is filling the bath), which, in its turn, is the Holy Grail. The Holy Grail, the empty vessel, is a symbol of the Principle and Meaning of Mary, and, as such, it is, therefore, ultimately a symbol of the heart as the dwelling-place of the 'image' and the 'likeness' of God. Here, the heart refers to the spiritual heart, the spiritual centre within each and every person; it is not the same as the physical heart, nor is it the emotional centre. The heart is thus the true and only Holy Grail and is, accordingly, a symbol of the Principle and Meaning of Mary. Mary is that place in which the 'image' and the 'likeness' of God dwells. Thus, Mary is the heart; she is the Holy Grail.

Hence, the women, the water, the bath, the vessel and the crib, (because it too is an open and, therefore, a receptive shape), are all symbols of the Holy Grail, and, therefore, of the heart, and, therefore, ultimately of the Principle and Meaning of Mary: of the means, that is, by which both births take place in the soul.

Furthermore, Mary unites and combines within herself between the midwife and the maid, thus symbolising the principle of Mind as Virgin and as Wife: that is, the pure reception and the pure transmission of the divine revelation in each instant, according to Itself, without any colouring whatsoever. This is what is symbolised by, for example, the halo in both Buddhist and Christian iconography; by Abraham and Sarah at the well of Mamre in icons of the Holy Trinity (Genesis 18.1); by the sister Goddesses Inanna and Ereshkigal of Sumerian mythology, and Isis and

Nephthys of Egyptian mythology (for sister Goddesses are not two separate Goddesses but, rather, two aspects of, two facets of, the same Goddess, the same Principle, the Principle and Meaning of Mary). It is also what is signified, in Sumerian mythology, by the six monthly alternation between this world and the underworld of Geshtinanna and her brother Dumuzi.

One of the women bearing gifts is carrying a spindle, another a vase and a third a tray (also the empty vessel) of food. As will be explored in more detail later, weaving, pottery making and baking were three crafts carried on in the temple during the Neolithic period because they all symbolise the Goddess as the source of birth and rebirth, and therefore, ultimately the Principle and Meaning of Mary.

Following the three young women bearing gifts is another carrying a fan of peacock feathers at the top of a staff. The staff is one from amongst the many symbols of the World Axis, and the World Axis is the link between Heaven and Earth, the spiritual and the material, the divine and the human and which, by uniting and combining within itself between them, proclaims their no-otherness; that is, it announces that God is the actuality and, therefore, the Truth, both of ourselves and of the whole of creation.

The staff is of two colours, dark and light blue, split down the middle. The two colours represent the two movements, the two currents of manifestation: the creative act, the bestowal of becoming (being on loan); the coming into manifestation, the descending, dismembering movement; the shattering and the splitting of lightning, the stone axe and the hammer of Thor, represented by Euphrosyne ('mirth', 'the bringer of joy', 'pleasure') of the Three Graces. The other movement being the ascending, the returning, the re-membering, symbolised by the rising of the fire of lightning, the stone axe and the hammer of Thor, represented also by Aglaia ('brightness', 'brilliance', 'beauty') of the Three Graces. The two movements, the two currents, are united in the staff, the Axis itself, as the third of the Three Graces, Thalia ('abundance') unites and combines within herself between Euphrosyne and Aglaia; as the Saint, by way of, and only by way of, Self-Gift unites and combines within herself or himself between the transcendent and the immanent, between the unity and the multiplicity, and, accordingly, witnesses the transcendent in the immanent and the immanent in the transcendent, the unity in the multiplicity and the multiplicity in the unity.

The same principle is also symbolised in, for example, Sandro Botticelli's painting of *The Birth of Venus* both by the fact that Aphrodite is on the shoreline (that is, at the junction of the two worlds) and that she is full-frontal nude (symbolising the interior) and yet she is about to be clothed: that is, veiled in the forms of the world, of manifestation, as she steps ashore. Other representations include the Caduceus of Hermes, the two faces of Isimud, the Sukkal (the Grand Vizier or chief minister) of Enki, the god of wisdom and water in Sumerian mythology, and the two faces of Janus in Classical mythology. And, just as in the staff the two colours are united in the staff itself, so both Isimud and Janus have an invisible third face, which unites and combines within itself between the two.[2]

God's Self-Gift is a single instantaneous act, but since God is infinite, the Gift is infinitely received, and since God never repeats Himself because He is infinite, both ourselves and the whole of creation return to Him in each instant to be recreated anew. This is what is meant by the so called 'destroyer' aspect of the Hindu Goddess Kali, simply, and nothing other than, our return to God and our recreation in each instant in Love and according to Beauty.

The Holy *Qur'an* says, 'God is now as He was' and yet 'every day He is in a new configuration'. The 'configuration' is the new creation in each instant, which is an unfoldment of that which lies within each individual *logos*; but, simultaneously, God 'is now as He was', for it is God Who manifests Himself in the 'new configuration' of the new creation, as the actuality of both ourselves and of the whole of creation. However, within Himself, the essence is unaffected by Self-Gift, so within Himself God 'is now as He was'. Thus, in each of the cases mentioned above, the two movements symbolise the 'new configuration' and the uniting and combining factor or principle, 'God is as He was'.

Whilst each of the above mentioned examples has, primarily, other meanings, in each case, essentially, they represent the union of the hidden and the manifest and that the one is hidden in the other; the manifest in the hidden (as source and actuality) and the hidden, as source and actuality, in the manifest, just as 'every day He is in a new configuration' is hidden in 'God is as He was' as source and actuality and 'God is as He was' is hidden, as source and actuality, in 'every day He is in a new configuration'.

The peacock is a symbol of incorruptibility, therefore of eternal life and, therefore, of the Resurrection, which expresses itself in this world in the belief that the flesh of the peacock is incorruptible. The 'eyes' on the tail of the peacock, (as also, the eyes of the eagle, the hawk, the owl, the bird of prey, the eyes of the fish and the deer, stars, and the eyes of Tiresias) symbolise the inner spiritual sight, the vision, that is, of the inner, spiritual Mind. The distinction between the spiritual Mind (*Nous*, in eastern Christian spirituality, *Apex Mentis*, in western) and the rational Mind (*Dianoia* or *Mens*) is a universal one. The spiritual Mind is situated in the heart, the spiritual centre and perceives the divine intuitively and without any intermediary. Accordingly, it is universally known as 'the eye of the heart'. Saint Paul says 'But we have the mind of Christ' (I Corinthians 2.16) and Saint Paul has 'the Mind of Christ' because Saint Paul, by dying to himself, has returned to the condition of his original creation and is, therefore, according to both the 'image' and the 'likeness' of God. The 'Mind of Christ' is the Divine Wisdom, God's Knowledge of Himself, the *Hagia Sophia*, which is symbolised by Enki in Sumerian mythology and by Athene in Classical mythology. If and when we have died to ourselves, which death can only take place as a result of the combination of our effort, the Principle and Meaning of Mary and Grace, then we too can indeed say with Saint Paul 'but we have the Mind of Christ' because we too can then say, with Saint Paul, 'I live; yet not I, but Christ liveth in me' (Galatians 2.20).

Titus Burckhardt has pointed out that whilst invisible in itself, light becomes visible through colour; and the richness of colour points to the inner richness of the 'primordial light' of the divine image which dwells in the heart.[3] Accordingly, the eyes on the peacock's tail do indeed symbolise the 'eye of the heart', which, by way of, and only by way of, Self-Gift, perceives both the inner richness of the primordial light itself and the richness in which the light manifests and reveals itself by way of colour; represented, in this case, by the vivid, brilliant colours on the peacock's tail and body. The peacock moults annually which, as also the snake shedding its skin, and hibernation, is a symbol of renewal and rejuvenation, of death and rebirth, of dying before we die; that is, it is a demonstration of the Principle and Meaning of Mary, by means of which we too can have the vision symbolised by the eyes on the tail of the peacock, because we too have 'the Mind of Christ'. Joseph Campbell has pointed out that the eyes on the tail of the peacock also symbolise 'the opening from within of the eyes of the ground of being, to view the universe of its own body'.[4]

The fan is in the shape of an inverted triangle. Because the inverted triangle is an open and, therefore, a receptive shape, because it is in the form of an empty cup or vessel, it is universally a symbol of sheer receptivity: of, that is, the Principle and Meaning of Mary. It is also the shape of the vulva, both according to its principial, primordial meaning

of the womb of creation, Prime Matter, sheer receptivity, the
Principle and Meaning of Mary; and in the sense that this
Principle manifests and reveals itself in the female sexual
and reproductive organs, the vulva and the womb.

Marija Gimbutas says that in the iconography of both
the Paleolithic and Neolithic periods the vulva is not just a
symbol of birth but also of death, but of death as, and only
as, rebirth; of returning via the Goddess's holy vulva to her
womb (the upper waters) to die and be reborn in the living
waters of the amniotic fluid of her womb: accordingly, it is
a symbol of the two births.[5]

At the apex of the triangle and the top of the staff, is
a circle from which both the triangle and the staff emerge
or proceed as from their source and origin. The circle,
whole and complete within itself, is a symbol of God as
the actuality of both ourselves and the whole of creation.
The centre represents the spiritual, the heavenly realms,
symbolised by the sky; the circumference the corporeal,
symbolised by the earth; and the space in between, the
intermediary psychic realms, symbolised by the air.

Saint Joachim is standing in a doorway, his head
bowed, his right hand on his chest, beholding the scene
within; that is, beholding within himself the spiritual
meaning of that which is taking place within the room,
just as the purpose of our mosaic is to direct us to our own
interiors wherein, and wherein alone, the meaning of that
which we are witnessing in the mosaic lies. That Saint
Joachim's head is bowed, (bowed, that is, in submission)
and his right hand is on his heart, (his heart, that is, as
spiritual centre), are themselves demonstrations of the
Principle and Meaning of Mary; and that Saint Joachim has
realised and fulfilled that Meaning within himself, which
is why he is able to contemplate the hidden meaning of
the mystery that is being revealed to him and which he is
contemplating within his own heart.

The door, like the gate, the window and the arch, is

an opening, a passageway between the two worlds (the interior and the exterior, the spiritual and the material, the divine and the human) but as no other than one another. That Saint Joachim is standing in the doorway, neither inside nor out, shows that he himself stands at the junction of the two worlds, and that he unites and combines within himself between the two; as Aphrodite in Sandro Botticelli's painting of *The Birth of Venus*, as Abraham sitting in the entrance to his tent at the Well of Mamre in icons of the Holy Trinity (Genesis 18.1), all unite and combine within themselves between the two, thereby demonstrating the same principle we are witnessing here in Saint Joachim standing in the doorway; thereby, again, directing us to our own interiors.

The door and the gate, as also the cave, the house, the palace, the temple and the room all represent the empty vessel, that is, they represent the Principle and Meaning of Mary and thus the heart as the dwelling-place of the 'image' and the 'likeness' of God. Accordingly, they also symbolise the body and the womb of the Goddess from which we are born and to which we return in death to be reborn. Because of this, eventually, the door, the gate, came to represent the whole structure—so that simply passing through the door or the gate came to symbolise death and rebirth, as is the case with the Japanese Torii.[6]

The doorway is in the form of a tower and fills almost the whole of the structure. The height of the doorway is in itself a symbol of spiritual elevation: that is, of the two births, as it is also an axial symbol. The summit of the tower, the doorway, is a triangle with curving sides, which is itself a symbol of the creative principle, and which was, originally, also a Goddess symbol, of the mountain as the body and the womb of the Goddess. Here, the apex of the triangle, the pyramid, represents the principial unity, the non-individuated state and the two arms, the two movements or currents of manifestation, whilst the base line represents the unfoldments of that which lies within the *logoi*. The two lower corners also represent the opposites, which are united, resolved and transcended in the apex, from which their unfoldments emerge as no other than it and to which they return. In the centre of the arch/pyramid formed by the gable end of the roof, there is a floral design with, at its centre, a rising stem which bears a striking resemblance to the head of a cobra, the serpent being a sacred animal of the Goddess, not the least because of its ability to shed its skin and because it hibernates, both of which are symbols of death and rebirth, which, accordingly, make it a symbol of the Principle and Meaning of Mary. The symbolism of the axis and the two movements or currents of manifestation is also present in this design which thus reflects the meaning of the whole structure, and, therefore of the heart as the dwelling-place of the 'image' and the 'likeness' of God.

Beginning at the doorway in which Saint Joachim is standing, and stretching across the whole of the background, is a red veil, which regularly appears in icons depicting scenes from Mary's life. Mary was one of the maidens chosen to weave the veil to cover the entrance to the Holy of Holies at the temple of Solomon in Jerusalem.[7] The true Holy of Holies is the heart as the dwelling-place of the 'image' of God, of which the Holy of Holies in the temple is a symbol; thus, as with the Holy Grail so the Holy of Holies is another symbolic representation of the Principle and Meaning of Mary and as Mary is the true Holy Grail, so is she the true Holy of Holies.

The veil covering the entrance to the Holy of Holies in the temple is a symbol of the veil of self, which Saint Benedict calls the *'obex'*, and which, by affirming ourselves, we place between ourselves and God—that is, between ourselves and God's own perfect image of Himself which dwells in the true Holy of Holies of our hearts. The veil which covered the entrance to the Holy of Holies in the temple was rent asunder at the time of the crucifixion

(Matthew 28.51; Mark 15.38; Luke 23.45), as the veil of self, the *obex* is rent asunder…but we shall return to these themes when we come to the mosaics of the Presentation of Mary into the Temple and the Crucifixion.

The purpose of the veil is to conceal, and, accordingly, its presence in icons of Mary is to show that there is a spiritual meaning hidden within the icon—as indeed there is in all icons—a meaning which lies behind the veil of self, the *obex*, hidden within our hearts, wherein, and wherein alone lies the true meaning of the icon and wherein, and wherein alone, we shall find that meaning, because therein dwells the image of God. The function therefore of both veil and icon is to direct us to our own interiors to discover and thus to realise and fulfil that meaning within ourselves.

It is equally true however, that the veil is the veil with and by means of which God veils Himself when, as Self-Gift, He manifests and reveals Himself by way of ourselves and the whole of creation, and this is the meaning of the veil in Sandro Botticelli's *The Birth of Venus*. The nudity of Aphrodite, in spiritual terms, represents the divine Love and Beauty, the Love and Beauty of God, essentially, in essence, divest of form, yet containing all forms within itself, according to its naked (of form) reality. Meister Eckhart speaks about seizing God in his wardrobe; we must, he says:

> Apprehend Him in the pure and naked substance where He is nakedly apprehending Himself. For goodness and justice are God's garment which covers Him. Therefore, strip God of all His clothing—seize Him naked in His robing-room, where He is uncovered and bare in Himself.[8]

The veil is the divine Love and Beauty manifesting and revealing Itself by way of the forms both of ourselves and of the whole of creation. But what lies behind the forms is the naked essence Itself, as Aphrodite is both full frontal nude (essence) and yet is about to be clothed in the veil of form as she steps ashore. Accordingly, the Saint, the one from whom, by way of the Principle and Meaning of Mary and Grace, the veil of self, the *obex*, has been removed, witnesses both the form and the naked reality behind the form, the essence: that is, the Saint witnesses the unity in the multiplicity and the multiplicity in the unity.

In Velázquez's painting *The Toilet of Venus* (also known as *The Rokeby Venus*), Aphrodite is lying nude on a bed, her back to us, looking at herself in a mirror. When the veil of self has been removed from us we are then able to seize God in His wardrobe, for then God has equally removed the veil from Himself, for then it is God seizing Himself in His wardrobe and, just as the painting shows, it is God, by way of Self-Gift, beholding Himself as He Himself is in us as His own perfect 'image' and 'likeness'.

Just as Mary gave birth to God in her soul before she gave birth to Christ, The Word, the 'image', in her womb, so did Saint Anna give birth to Mary in her soul before she gave birth to Mary in her womb. 'Mystery goes before greater mystery; the sterile door is opened and the virginal door comes forth' as the Liturgy of the Orthodox Church affirms in the celebration of the festival of the birth of Mary (September 8th); which, in its turn, means that, as Leonid Ouspensky says, 'It is our nature which ceases to be sterile and which starts to bear the fruits of grace'.[9] So must we give birth to Mary in our souls. But the awesome mystery and wonder of this sublime paradox is, as Origen says, that by giving birth to Mary in our souls, we thereby make Mary our mother too, and by making Mary our mother too is meant that we realise and fulfil within ourselves the Principle and Meaning of Mary.[10] Whilst we shall return to this theme again when we come to the mosaics of the Annunciation and the Crucifixion, what happens when we give birth to Mary in our souls, thereby making Mary our mother too, is that the Second Birth takes place within us and our souls are born back into God. It is then, as Leonid Ouspensky observes, that our nature ceases to be sterile and we too start to bear 'the fruits of grace' in that we then allow God to appear in us and to act in us as Himself in us as His own perfect 'image' and 'likeness'.

As Dom Sylvester says, we are all the House of God, the *Domus Dei*, the *Baytu-llâh*, which is also the Household of God and we are the House of God because, by way of Self-Gift, we are the dwelling-place of God's own perfect image of Himself as He Himself is. We are, therefore, equally, the Palace in which God, the Divine ruler, dwells as we are also the true Temple of God.

Whilst we are the House of God, we are not necessarily the Household of God since, for so long as we claim the House for ourselves we thereby determine over God by compelling Him to appear in us and to act in us as ourselves in us as in His own perfect image only. However, as Dom Sylvester says, our spiritual progress consists in the return from being the House of God (First Birth) into being also the Household of God (Second Birth) in which God carries out His chores.[11]

As the means, together with Grace, whereby both births take place, Mary is, accordingly, the mistress of the House, the Queen of the Palace and the High Priestess of the Temple, as she is also the House, the Palace, the Temple itself. It is perhaps worth bearing in mind that 'Queen of the Palace' was one of the epithets of the Sumerian Goddess Inanna, whose name means 'Queen of Heaven', as Mary is the 'Queen of Heaven', and that the name of the Egyptian Goddess Nephthys (Nebthet or Nebhet in Egyptian and sister-self of Isis) means 'Mistress of the Palace', 'Lady of the House'.[12]

In the opening of the sterile and the coming forth of the virginal we have the 'barren', 'sterile' woman of Philo of Alexandria, and Psalm 113. 9, who is the mother of many children, representing, once more, Mind as Virgin and as Wife: for if, as Philo says, we are alive to ourselves, then we are 'dead', that is, we are 'sterile and barren' with regard to God, but, if we are alive to God then we are 'dead', that is, we are 'sterile and barren' with regard to ourselves. We are empty, that is, of ourselves and, therefore, we allow God to appear in us and to act in us as Himself in us as His own perfect 'image' and 'likeness', which, in its turn, means that the divine revelation is received and transmitted (that is, expressed in action) in each instant according to its purity. Thus, we are the barren, sterile woman who is the mother of many children.[13] Which means that Mind is both Virgin and a Wife, since, being empty of ourselves, we are now both the House and the Household of God in which God carries out His chores.

This is also one of the meanings of Artemis, the Virgin Goddess huntress who is no other than Mary. As Artemis is an embodiment of the principle of spiritual and cosmological Virginity and, accordingly, of Divine Motherhood (both cosmologically as Prime Matter and spiritually as Mind as Virgin and as Wife)), the connection between Artemis and Mary is particularly close. Thus, she is associated with Nature in its natural, uncultivated state, symbolising, thereby, the Virgin soul untouched by the self, which has been removed from it. Laurens van der Post says that hunting symbolises the search, the quest for ever deeper, for ever greater meaning: that is, the search, the quest within for ever deeper, for ever greater meaning.[14] Everything in creation is a 'word' of God, and, accordingly, each and every animal and plant is a revelation of, a manifestation of, a spiritual meaning and principle, which principle, which meaning, that animal, that plant, manifests and expresses completely in every single mode of its existence: thus, these animals (in hunting) represent the ever greater and deeper meanings and principles, the search for which, the quest for which, the act of hunting itself symbolises (hence the Goddess as the *Potnia Theron*, the Mistress of the animals, because she, as source, contains all those principles and meanings within herself).

Artemis, the Virgin Goddess is equally Ephesian Artemis of the many eggs, which symbolise, because of her meaning, as Prime Matter, the eternal essences (the *logoi*) of all that exists by way of becoming, as they also symbolise the fertility of the whole of creation and, especially, spiritual fertility, which is the fertility of Heart of Mind, expressed in the movement from the interior to the exterior as Mind as Virgin and as Wife and which, in both senses, is the Divine Motherhood. Thus, in Artemis we have another demonstration of the spiritual Mind, Heart of Mind, which dwells in the heart which Mary is, hunting, preying upon, feeding upon the ever deeper, the ever greater meanings of the Divine realities hidden within the Divine Wisdom.

According to tradition, at the Crucifixion Christ entrusted Mary to Saint John who, subsequently, took Mary with him to Ephesus, where she remained for the rest of her life here on earth. Ephesus was the site of the greatest temple of Artemis, which temple was one of the Seven Wonders of the World. In coming to Ephesus, Mary was completing and sealing the Principle of which Artemis was herself an expression and of which Mary is the supreme expression. Mary did not come to Ephesus to deny Artemis but, rather, to affirm, complete and seal her meaning.

It was at Ephesus, in 431, that the Second Ecumenical Council of the Christian Church proclaimed that the title of *Theotokos* ('She who gives birth to God') does indeed belong to Mary, as indeed, from a spiritual perspective, it does, for it is by way of the Principle and Meaning of Mary, together with Grace, that both the First and the Second Births take place within the soul. Joseph Campbell says that whilst the Council was in progress 'the people of Ephesus formed picket lines and shouted in praise of Mary, "the Goddess, the Goddess, of course she's the Goddess"'.[15]

Saint Anna is sitting up on her bed, looking at Mary. The bed and bedchamber are symbols of the heart as the dwelling-place of the 'image' and the 'likeness' of God. Our access to that bedchamber, in which Saint Anna gave birth to Mary and into which she took Mary after the first seven steps, depends, as Saint Gregory of Nyssa says, upon whether we rest in God or in ourselves. If we rest in ourselves, by so doing we determine over God by compelling Him to appear in us and to act in us as ourselves in us as His own perfect image, and, therefore, access to the chamber (of our hearts) is denied to us. If however, we rest in God, then, by being 'asleep' to ourselves we are 'awake' to God; that is, we are empty of ourselves and because we are empty of ourselves we allow God to appear in us and to act in us as Himself in us as His own perfect 'image' and 'likeness' and we are, accordingly, admitted into the bedchamber.[16] This is so, Saint Gregory says, even when we are physically asleep, for then the heart never sleeps, as both Philo and the Prophet Mohammad also say.[17] We can only be admitted into the bedchamber of our hearts, the chamber in which Saint Anna gave birth to Mary, by giving birth to Mary in our souls, thereby making Mary our mother too, and, thereby, making Mary the Queen and Mistress of the bedchamber of our hearts.

Notes

1 *The Protevangelium of James,* and *The Gospel Of Pseudo-Matthew,* included in Ante-Nicene Fathers vol. VIII. Ed. by The Rev. Alexander Roberts D.D. and James Donaldson LL.D. (Edinburgh: T&T Clark; Grand Rapids, Michigan: Wm. B. Eerdmans Publishing, 1989 Repr.), *Protevangelium,* chapter 4, p.362. *Pseudo-Matthew,* chapter 2, p.369 and chapter 3, p.370.

2 For the invisible third face of Janus see René Guénon,

Fundamental Symbols: The Universal Language of Sacred Science (Cambridge, England: Quinta Essentia, 1st English transl. 1995; repr. undated), pp.90-91.

[3] Titus Burckhardt, *Chartres and the Birth of the Cathedral* English Edition (Ipswich, England: Golgonooza Press, 1995), p.105; and, *Sacred Art in East and West* (Louisville, Kentucky: Fons Vitae, 1st American edn 2001), p.202.

[4] Joseph Campbell, *The Masks of God*, 4 vols (London: Souvenir Press (Educational and Academic Ltd.), 2001), IV Creative Mythology, pp.501-3.

[5] Marija Gimbutas, *The Language of the Goddess* (London: Thames and Hudson, 1st paperback edn 2001), chapter 12 pp.99-111 and chapter 21, pp.237-245.

[6] For the door/gate as the Holy Vulva and Womb of the Goddess see: Erich Neumann, *The Great Mother*, Bollingen Series XLVII (Princeton, N.J.: Princeton University Press, 7th paperback printing 1991), pp. 46, 158-9 and 282-3. For the Japanese Torii see Titus Burckhardt, *Sacred Art in East and West*, p. 103 footnote. See also G. R. Levy, *The Gate of Horn* (London: Faber and Faber, 1948; repr. 1963), pp.100 & 127.

[7] *The Protevangelium of James*, chapter 10, p.363.

[8] *Meister Eckhart Sermons and Treatises*, trans. and ed. by M. O'C. Walshe, 4 vols (Longmead, Shaftesbury, Dorset: Element Books, 2nd impression, 1989), II, Sermon 63, pp.117-8.

[9] Leonid Ouspensky and Vladimir Lossky, *The Meaning of Icons* (Crestwood, New York: St. Vladimir's Seminary Press), p.146.

[10] *Origen: Commentary on the Gospel of John*, included in Ante-Nicene Fathers, 5th Edn, vol. X. Ed. by Allan Menzies (Edinburgh: T&T Clark and Grand Rapids, Michigan: Wm. B. Eerdmans Publishing Company, Repr. 1990), p.300.

[11] Dom Sylvester Houédard, 'The Golden Bricks Of Ibn 'Arabi',

Journal of the Muhyiddin Ibn 'Arabi Society, 8 (1989), 50-58 (pp.50 & 52).

[12] Diane Wolkstein and Samuel Noah Kramer, *Inanna Queen of Heaven and Earth* (New York: Harper and Row, 1983), pp.xvi, 34 and 39.

[13] G.R.S. Mead, *Thrice Greatest Hermes: Studies in Hellenistic Theosophy and Gnosis*, 3 vols (No place of publication given. Originally published by the Theosophical Publishing Society, 1906. This edition by Kessinger Publishing (Rare Mystical Reprints), no date), I, pp.154-5.

[14] Laurens van der Post, *A Mantis Carol* (London: Hogarth Press, 1975), p.18.

[15] Joseph Campbell in conversation with Bill Moyers, *The Power of Myth* (New York: Anchor Books, Doubleday, 1988), p.224.

[16] Saint Gregory of Nyssa, *From Glory to Glory: Texts from Gregory of Nyssa's Mystical Writings*. Selected and with an introduction by Jean Daniélou, S.J. Trans. and ed. by Herbert Musurillo, S.J. (Crestwood, New York: St. Vladimir's Seminary Press, 1979), pp.240-2.

[17] G.R.S. Mead, I, p.148.

THE FIRST SEVEN STEPS
OF MARY

hen Mary was six months old, Saint Anna 'put her on the ground to try whether she could stand, and she walked seven steps and came into her bosom'.[1]

In the mosaic, Mary is shown walking towards Saint Anna, who is sitting on a stool with a footstool attached. Behind Mary is a woman with a shawl arching over her head. Two wings extend from either side of the background architecture. Behind the structure, at the point where each wing emerges from the central bay, is a tree. The veil is also present, this time just the two ends hanging over the gable end of each bay. David Talbot Rice says that the shawl over the head of the woman behind Mary 'derives from an old Classical motif usually associated with personifications'.[2] In other words, she is not there! She thus represents the First Birth, the birth of God into the soul, which is the spiritual First Coming of Christ; whilst Saint Anna symbolises our return to that condition, which is the Second Birth, the birth of the soul back into God, which is the spiritual meaning of the Second Coming of Christ.

Mary is exactly midway between the two, showing thereby that the woman behind her and Saint Anna are both facets of, aspects of, the Principle and Meaning of

Mary and that both births take place within the soul by way of the combination of the Principle and Meaning of Mary and Grace; and that Mary unites and combines within herself between the two births, as, indeed, does Saint Anna and all those who, by giving birth to Mary in their souls, thereby making Mary their mother too, and in whom, accordingly, the Second Birth has taken place. The same is also demonstrated both by the pose and the position, in relation to the architectural setting, of both Saint Anna and the figure behind Mary, each of whom is positioned before one of the two projecting wings (the two Births), each with her head bowed towards the centre, where Mary is.

Seven is the number of Mary, because seven is the virgin number, and seven is the virgin number because, as Philo of Alexandria says, alone of the numbers from one to ten, seven is neither 'engendered' nor does it 'engender'. Four, for example, is both 'engendered' (2x2), and 'engenders', (2x4=8).[3] As the virgin number, seven is, accordingly, the number of Mary and, therefore, of the Goddess, who is one but whose names are many and who is no other than Mary.

The Buddha took seven steps upon attaining enlightenment, and the number also occurs in Sumerian mythology in the Descent of Inanna. 'From the Great Above', Inanna, the Queen of Heaven (and Earth, both of which are epithets of Mary) opened her Mind to the 'Great Below':

> My Lady abandoned Heaven and Earth to descend to the underworld. Inanna abandoned Heaven and Earth to descend to the underworld. She abandoned her office of holy priestess to descend to the underworld.[4]

The underworld is the interior, the inner spiritual world. So the descent to the underworld represents the inner spiritual journey to Heart of Mind which is the *Kenosis* of Christian mysticism; and, accordingly, Ereshkigal is the principle of spiritual death which gives birth to the Virgin Wife Inanna in the soul.

Before beginning her descent to her sister self, Ereshkigal, Inanna visited seven of her temples, situated throughout Sumer, north, south, east and west; she abandoned, that is, everywhere and everything. In the course of her descent, Inanna passed through seven gates, and at each gate an item of clothing was removed from her by Neti, the Chief Gatekeeper of the Kur, the underworld, until by the time she had passed through the seventh and final gate, she was nude; nude, because she has abandoned everywhere and everything, including, most of all, herself. Thus, she is, symbolically, showing us the pure naked Virgin soul which Mary is, empty of the self, and, therefore receiving Self-Gift as It is given, according to Its purity. Ereshkigal fastened upon Inanna 'the eye of death. She spoke against her the word of wrath. She uttered against her the cry of guilt' and, 'Inanna was turned into a corpse, A piece of rotting meat, And was hung from a hook on the wall'.[5]

Briefly, Inanna, like Christ, was three days dead and then resurrected. Joseph Campbell says that the Descent of Inanna is the 'earliest extant example' of the 'Dance of the Seven Veils', which dance is the symbolic 'stripping of the self'.[6] In the Descent of Inanna we also have a demonstration of the spiritual meaning of the Raising of Lazarus (John 11. 1-46), and that the words 'Lazarus come forth' are addressed to all of us; to all of us, that is, who are not Saints. In order to emerge from the tomb, we must be spiritually 'alive' and in order to be spiritually 'alive', we must be 'alive' to God; in order to be 'alive' to God, we must be 'dead' to ourselves: we must 'die before we die'. In order to 'die before we die', we must realise and fulfil within ourselves the meaning of the First Seven Steps of Mary, that is, of the Principle and Meaning of Mary, of which realisation and fulfilment, the Descent of Inanna is a manifestation.

Mary was six months old. Six, the sixth day of Genesis (Genesis 1. 24-31), is the number of our original creation as according to both the 'image' and the 'likeness' of God, because six is the double Trinity: the Trinity *'ad intra'* and the Trinity *'ad extra'*, that is God as He always and forever is within Himself and God manifesting and revealing Himself to Himself as Himself in the movement of Self-Gift which is the Holy Spirit. Accordingly, six is the first perfect number—a number which is equal to both the sum and the product of its factors: 1+2+3=6 and 1x2x3=6.[7] Further, six months is half a year and half a year is half a cycle, which is again why Mary is exactly half way between the female figure behind her, and Saint Anna; the cycle is completed by way of the meaning of the seven, by way that is, of the Meaning of the one who is making the journey, so that Self-Gift may be received as It was given at our original creation, whole and entire. We are being shown, and being shown by Mary herself, that, as Saint Gregory Nazianzos says (see Introduction), in order to receive ourselves entire we must give ourselves entire. Mary is showing us both the way and the means whereby our souls may be born back into God.

Saint Anna is sitting on a footstool, and the stool, the seat, the chair and the throne are all revelations of the Principle and Meaning of Mary. In Christian iconography, Christ is shown seated upon the lap of Mary; Mary, that is, is the throne upon which Christ sits, just as, in Egyptian iconography, Horus is shown seated upon the lap of Isis, for Isis is the throne upon which Horus sits. Isis, because and only because she is no other than Mary, is the embodiment, the personification of the throne so that she is frequently depicted wearing the hieroglyph for the throne on her head and her name, in Egyptian, Asset/Ast or Esset/Est, means 'seat' or 'throne'. In Sumerian mythology Inanna wanted the 'throne and the bed', and earlier still, the throne was a Goddess symbol.[8]

The throne of the Goddess is, therefore, the throne of Inanna, is the throne of which Isis is the embodiment and personification, is the primeval throne of Egyptian mythology, is the throne supported by eight angels (the eight directions of space—the four cardinal directions and the four intermediate points) which encompasses the totality of manifestation of the Holy *Qur'an*, is the empty chair at the top of the mimbar in mosques, is the lotus floating upon the surface of the primeval ocean, is the empty throne of Byzantium, Buddhism and Hinduism, and which symbolises the presence of the unseen ruler, Who is the one who stands amongst us and whom we know not of Saint John the Baptist (John 1.26), both in ourselves and in the whole of creation.[9] That is, it symbolises the presence of God as actuality both in ourselves and in the whole of creation. And that which receives the presence of the unseen ruler, both in ourselves and in the whole of creation, that which receives the presence of God as actuality, both in ourselves and in the whole of creation is the Principle and Meaning of Mary.

Isis is the throne upon which Horus sits; that is, Isis is the place which receives and gives birth to the presence of Horus, just as Mary is the throne upon which Christ sits. That is, Mary is the place which receives and gives birth to the presence of Christ, both literally and spiritually. So when we look at a mosaic of Christ seated upon the lap of Mary, we are actually looking at ourselves, at our hearts as according to the condition of our original creation; and, if and when, by giving birth to Mary in our souls, thereby making Mary our mother too, we return to that condition, then we are looking at ourselves as we are now. But, first, we too must sit upon the lap of Mary 'as a child upon its mother's lap'.

Accordingly, Joseph Campbell says that the pharaoh (in ancient Egypt) seated upon his throne is the pharaoh sitting upon the lap of Isis 'as a child upon its mother's lap'.[10] Mary, the Principle and Meaning of Mary, is the supreme expression of the principle of the seat, the chair, the throne; for Mary is the seat, the chair, the throne of the heart as the dwelling-place of the image of God. So, here in our mosaic, Saint Anna sitting upon the stool is Saint Anna sitting upon the lap of Mary 'as a child upon its mother's lap', for Saint Anna has given birth to Mary in her soul, thereby making Mary her mother too. Which is further symbolised by Saint Anna receiving Mary into 'her bosom', that is, into her heart.

Saint Anna's feet are resting upon a footstool, which is attached to the stool/chair upon which she is sitting. In that the feet are the point of contact with the ground, they can represent the affirmation of the world perceived by the senses (as opposed to the affirmation of the world as it actually is as manifesting and revealing God). Accordingly, they represent the affirmation of the separate self, which is the spiritual meaning of sloth; the slothful being those who are slow to affirm God and, therefore, swift to affirm themselves. However, as Saint Dionysios the Areopagite says, the feet can also represent 'swiftness and progress' in the affirmation of God,[11] which, Saint Gregory of Nyssa says in his exposition on the meaning of the Beatitudes, is the spiritual meaning of the Beatitude 'Blessed are the meek'. The 'meek' of the Beatitude, Saint Gregory says, are those in whom the movement to otherness is slow; that is, they are slow to affirm themselves and, therefore, they are swift to affirm God.[12]

Thus, Mary is always shown either with tiny feet, as in our mosaic, or her feet are not shown at all, and the Saints are frequently shown either with bare feet or, as Saint Anna in our mosaic, with their feet not touching the ground. For, as Saint Gregory of Nyssa says 'sandaled feet cannot ascend that height where the light of truth is seen' so the covering of dead skins 'must be removed from the feet of the soul'.[13] The covering of dead skins covering the 'feet of the soul' represents the affirmation of the separate self which can only be removed from 'the feet of the soul' by way of a combination of the Principle and Meaning of Mary and Grace.

The architectural setting for our mosaic, as for all mosaics (icons) in which architecture features forms, as Leonid Ouspensky says, a backdrop only against which the event depicted takes place, for the event in question does not take place inside the building, but in front of it, which demonstrates, thereby, that whilst we are beholding an event which did indeed happen in a particular place at a certain point in time, the event itself, as well as its meaning and its relevance, are not circumscribed by place and time, for it is an inner spiritual event, with an inner spiritual meaning which is eternally occurring within the soul and, therefore, its meaning and its relevance is and are for all places and all times.[14] The house is the house that 'Wisdom hath builded for herself' (Proverbs 9.1), which house is the *Domus Dei*, the *Baytu-llâh*, the heart as the dwelling-place of the 'image' and the 'likeness' of God. Accordingly, the architecture is really the spiritual 'architecture' of the heart, which is what the physical architecture is, in fact, showing us and that, as such, its meaning is a spiritual meaning which can only be comprehended by the inner spiritual Mind: in other words, in order to comprehend it, with Saint Paul, we too must have 'the mind of Christ' (I Corinthians 2.16) and we can only have 'the mind of Christ' by realising and fulfilling within ourselves the meaning the architecture is showing to us: the Principle and Meaning of Mary. The architecture is showing us 'silently and by way of representation', as Saint Basil the Great says, what the Prophet Mohammad and Christ (and the Buddha, and all the prophets and sages and Saints of all religions) are saying to us in words: that is, to be what is being shown (said) to us we must 'die before we die'; we must 'die' to ourselves. As Inanna in her descent from 'the Great Above to the Great Below', so we too must abandon everywhere and everything; we must, that is, abandon ourselves as we perceive ourselves to be, and in her descent Inanna is showing us the meaning of the spiritual death to self, of 'dying before we die'. The purpose, whether the meaning is being presented to us 'silently and by way of representation', or in the form of the spoken or written word, is always to point us to our own interiors wherein, and wherein alone, the meaning lies and wherein, and wherein alone, it will be found, realised and fulfilled.

The two trees are axial symbols, thereby uniting and combining within themselves all the realms. Which symbolism is further emphasised, in the tree, by the leaves, the twigs, the branches all emerging from a central source, the trunk: God, that is, as the actuality of both ourselves and of the whole of creation; for, as Christ says 'I am the vine and ye are the branches' (John 15.1-5). It is because of this that wood is a symbol of Prime Matter, and, therefore, of the Principle and Meaning of Mary. Green symbolises growth and regrowth and, therefore death and rebirth; for which reason it is universally the colour of the Spirit. Thus, in the tree (trees) we also have a symbol of the spiritual elevation (as in Saint Joachim's tower-doorway), which follows the death to self, and the subsequent restoration of the lost 'likeness' to the 'image'.

A window in the form of an arch is situated in the centre of the central bay. The window, together with the door, the gate and the arch, is an opening between the two worlds, but as no other than one another. The shape is again a Goddess symbol; a symbol, that is, of the Holy Vulva of the Goddess as the fount of birth and rebirth and therefore of the Principle and Meaning of Mary.

Throughout the Middle Ages, one of the epithets of Mary was 'Gate of Heaven'. At the top of the arch window is a projection in the form of a knob, which stands for the Omphalos, the World Navel, again representing both birth and rebirth and, therefore, once again, Mary.[15] Below the window is a horizontal line with, but not attached to it, a vertical line beneath it, thus forming an abbreviated cross. (The symbolism of the cross will be examined in chapter 7.)

On each bay there is a rectangle inside of which is a vertical line above a V (vulva) shape, below which is a horizontal line, beneath which is a pyramid. The rectangle (the four Cardinal directions) is a symbol of the cosmos emerging from the Holy Vulva of the Goddess (Mary) under the Gift, which is the Holy Spirit (the vertical), the horizontal representing the unfoldments of that which lies within the *logoi*.

For us to realise and fulfil within ourselves the meaning which is here being shown to us 'silently and by way of representation' we must take the first seven steps of Mary; that is, we must realise and fulfil within ourselves the meaning of the seven, by giving birth to Mary in our souls, thereby making Mary our mother too.

Notes

[1] *Protevangelium of James*, chapter 6, p.362.

[2] David Talbot Rice, *Art of the Byzantine Era* (London: Thames and Hudson, Repr. 1986), pp.79 & 228.

[3] *Philo of Alexandria: Selected Writings*, trans. and introduced by David Winston. The Classics of Western Spirituality Series (Ramsey, N.J.: Paulist Press, 1981), p.85

[4] Diane Wolkstein and Samuel Noah Kramer, *Inanna Queen of Heaven and Earth*, pp.52-73.

5 Ibid. p.60.

6 Joseph Campbell, *The Masks of God*, vol. IV, Creative Mythology, p. 104.

7 *Philo of Alexandria: Selected Writings*, p.106.

8 Diane Wolkstein and Samuel Noah Kramer, *Inanna Queen of Heaven and Earth*, pp.4-9.

9 Erich Neumann, *The Great Mother*, pp. 98-100.

10 Joseph Campbell with Bill Moyers, *The Power of Myth*, p.222.

11 Saint Dionysios the Areopagite, *The Celestial Hierarchies*. In Mystical Theology and The Celestial Hierarchies. Trans. by the Editors Of The Shrine Of Wisdom (Fintry, Brook, Nr. Godalming, Surrey, England: The Shrine Of Wisdom, 2nd edn 1965), p.64.

12 Saint Gregory of Nyssa, *The Lord's Prayer, The Beatitudes*. Trans. and annotated by Hilda C. Graef. Ancient Christian Writers Series No. 18 (New York: Newman Press (Paulist Press), 1954), Sermon 2, pp.97-105.

13 Saint Gregory of Nyssa, *The Life of Moses*. Trans. Introduction and Notes by Abraham J. Malherbe and Everett Ferguson. Preface by John Meyendorff (New York: The Classics of Western Spirituality. Paulist Press, 1978), p.59. See also: Richard Temple, *Icons And The Mystical Origins Of Christianity* (Longmead, Shaftesbury: Element Books, 1990), p.133.

14 For further information on architecture in icons see Leonid Ouspensky, *Theology of the Icon*, volume 1, pp. 189-191 and Richard Temple, *Icons And The Mystical Origins Of Christianity*, pp.139-141, 145-147 & 161-162.

15 For the Omphalos see Marija Gimbutas, *Language of the Goddess*, pp. 148-9, 158, 225 & 324.

THE PRESENTATION OF MARY INTO THE TEMPLE

aint Anna and Saint Joachim presented Mary into the 'temple of the Lord', when she was three years old. She remained in the temple, where angels fed her, until she was twelve.[1] In our mosaic, Mary is shown being presented to the high priest, Zachariah (the father of Saint John the Baptist), by Saint Anna and Saint Joachim. Behind Zachariah is the altar. The temple is circular and Mary is again shown beneath a ciborium at the top of three steps, where she is being offered food by an angel.

The presentation into the temple represents leaving behind the cares of the world and of the self, leaving behind the world perceived by the physical senses; that is, it symbolises leaving behind the affirmation of the self and, accordingly, the entry into our own interiors, the inner journey to Heart of Mind which is the *Kenosis* of Christian spirituality. This is so because, as Saint Paul tells us, we are the 'true temple of God' (I Corinthians 3.16); and we are 'the true temple of God' because, by way of Self-Gift, we are the dwelling-place of God's own perfect image of Himself.

Kenosis means being empty of ourselves; it is, therefore, the process whereby that separate self, the *obex* of Saint

Benedict, is removed from us by the combination of the Principle and Meaning of Mary, Grace and our effort. This, in its turn, is the 'belittling of ourselves' of Origen, who says, in his *Commentary on the Gospel of Saint Matthew*, that the children (Matthew 18. 1-6), 'the little ones' are the ones who belittle themselves,[2] which 'self' is the 'woman taken in adultery' of Saint John (John 8. 3-11). This 'belittling' is, Meister Eckhart says, the meaning of humility: 'the naughting and the rejecting of self'.[3] For, as Saint Maximos Confessor says in his *Commentary on the Lord's Prayer*, the humble man is the one who knows that being is not his, it is his on loan.[4] This process whereby we are emptied of ourselves is, Origen says, the symbolic driving out of the merchants, the moneylenders, the moneychangers, from the true temple of God, our souls (John 2. 14-16).[5]

Mary gave birth to God in her soul before she gave birth to Christ, the Word, the Image of God, in her womb. This process whereby Mary gave birth to God in her soul is demonstrated in our mosaic by the fact that she is shown twice; entering the temple and also in the Holy of Holies. Even though she was but three years old, Mary did not look back, but willingly and joyfully in complete submission, the complete submission to God which is her meaning, entered the temple, the true temple of her own interior, and mounted the steps. By means of which, we are being shown both that we too must enter the true temple, the temple of our interiors and how we must enter into it; that we may only enter that temple by way of the Principle and Meaning of Mary.

Mary is also showing us that whilst God does indeed 'thirst to be thirsted for', as both Saint Gregory Nazianzos (full quote and references given in the Introduction) and the Prophet Mohammad say, for there is a *Hadīth qudsi* of the Prophet in which God says 'My yearning for them is greater by far than their yearning for me'. Since God gives Himself to Himself as Himself as and in Love, we must want Him, long for Him, yearn for Him too, for, as Bulent Rauf said of the above mentioned *Hadīth*, 'we must prove Him wrong'.

This longing, this yearning, is, at its highest level, the *Eros* of Christian spirituality and of Greek mythology. *Eros*, as Dom Sylvester says, is selfish love; selfish because it proceeds from the self, for it is we who yearn to be selfless, and for so long as there is a self in us, even a self which yearns to be selfless, we can never be selfless. However, as Dom Sylvester also says, as Saint Gregory of Nyssa says in his *Commentary on the Beatitudes*, the paradox is resolved by the fact that this yearning, this *Eros*, is the mourning of the Beatitude 'Blessed are they that mourn' (Matthew 5. 3) and, as Beatitude Himself promises, those who mourn thus 'shall be comforted' and shall be comforted by Comfort Itself, that is, they shall be comforted by the Holy Spirit,[6] in that, together with the Principle and Meaning of Mary and *Eros*, the separate self is, accordingly, removed from us and *Eros* is thereby transformed, by the Comforter Who is the Holy Spirit, into *Agape*.

Thus, whilst we can never be selfless as long as a separate self remains within us, without that yearning and longing, the separate self can never be removed either, for it is by way of the combination of the Principle and Meaning of Mary and our effort (yearning, longing, mourning, *Eros*) that we are able to receive the comfort of Grace, whereby our selfish love is transformed, through the removal of the *obex*, into selfless love, into *Agape*. Then it is no longer a matter, as formerly, of our loving God with our love, but of God loving Himself with His Love, the Love which He is, in Himself in us as His own perfect 'image' and 'likeness'.

The moment in which *Eros* is transformed into *Agape* is the subject of Agnolo Bronzino's masterpiece, *Allegory of Love* (also known as *Venus with Cupid, an Allegory*) in the National Gallery in London. It is also one of the meanings of the Descent of Inanna.

The place where Mary lived in the temple is identified both in the Liturgy of the Orthodox Churches and in the writings of the Church Fathers as the Holy of Holies, and Zachariah put Mary in the Holy of Holies because he recognised that Mary herself is the true Holy of Holies; for Mary is the heart, which is the dwelling-place of the 'image' and the 'likeness' of God.

The temple is circular, as is the Holy of Holies in which Mary is sitting. The circle with its centre as origin and which gives birth to the whole infinity of creation, which emerges from it as no other than it and to which it returns to die and be reborn; thus, Mary is sitting amidst demonstrations of her meaning, for the very shape itself is a symbol of the Principle and Meaning which is supremely embodied in Mary herself, and of which Mary is the sealing expression.

The Holy of Holies consists of a domed roof resting upon four pillars. The dome is a universal symbol of heaven, as the four pillars, representing the four cardinal directions, are universal symbols of manifestation, and, at the centre, the heart, sits Mary, for Mary is the heart.

Mary being fed by angels shows that Mary is nourished to the full by God, and Mary is nourished to the full by God because Mary is empty of herself, and because Mary is empty of herself, she is filled to the full with God; that is, Mary allows God to appear in her and to act in her as Himself in her as in His own perfect 'image' and 'likeness'. For the same reason, Mary nourishes God to the full.

This nourishment to the full, which is the experience of God as He Himself is, directly, immediately, intuitively, without any intermediary, which is God experiencing Himself as He Himself is in us now as in His own perfect 'image' and 'likeness', is referred to in the language of mysticism as 'Taste' (*Dhawq*, in Arabic). This is the nourishment, the 'Taste', of Deuteronomy 8. 3: 'man doth not live by bread only, but by every *word* that proceedeth out of the mouth of the Lord doth man live'.

In his exposition of this text, Philo says that by means of it we are being shown that the Saints are nourished both by the whole Word, here symbolised by the 'mouth of the Lord', and by each and every part of the Word, here symbolised by 'each and every word' (that is, the *logoi*) 'that proceedeth out of the mouth of the Lord',[7] because the Saints perceive, directly, immediately, intuitively, without any intermediary, the Word in the words and the words in the Word; that is, they perceive the Unity in the multiplicity and the multiplicity in the Unity.

This, Origen says, is the inner meaning of the words in the Lord's Prayer rendered into English as 'give us this day our daily bread'. The Greek '*ton arton ton epiousion*' refers, he says, to bread for our Being, that is, to the Word Who is also the 'image', given to us as becomings, and in saying these words we are simultaneously affirming that we exist as, and only as, becomings actualised by Self-Gift and asking to die to self so that we may be empty of ourselves and, therefore, filled to the full with God, so that we too may be nourished both by the whole Word and by each and every part of it, as Philo says.[8] This, Saint Basil the Great says, is the spiritual meaning of fasting, which means not feeding upon and, therefore, not being nourished by, ourselves, for, by so doing, we cease to compel God to appear in us and to act in us as ourselves in us as in His own perfect 'image' only (which is the spiritual meaning of gluttony). Thus, by truly fasting, that is, by making Mary our mother too, we die to self and, accordingly, allow God to appear in us and to act in us as Himself in us as in His own perfect 'image' and 'likeness'.[9]

Our mosaic is showing us both that such 'Taste' is indeed possible for us too, and the means, by making Mary our mother too, whereby that possibility is realised and fulfilled within us, so that we, too, nourish God to the full and are nourished to the full by Him.

Notes

1. (a)*The Protevangelium of James*, 7.8, pp. 362-3 and (b) *The Gospel of Pseudo-Matthew* 4.8, pp.370-1.

2. Origen, Nicene Fathers edn, op. cit., pp.486-7.

3. Meister Eckhart, Sermon 74, p. 200.

4. Saint Maximos Confessor, *On The Lord's Prayer*. In (a) *The Philokalia: The Complete Text*, Trans. from the Greek and ed. by G.E.H. Palmer, Philip Sherrard and Kallistos Ware, 5 vols, (London: Faber & Faber, repr. 1984), ii, p.297 and (b) *Maximos Confessor: Selected Writings*. Trans. by George C. Berthold. The Classics Of Western Spirituality, (New Jersey: Paulist Press 1985), p. 111.

5. Origen, *Commentary On John*, p. 394.

6. Saint Gregory of Nyssa, *The Beatitudes*, p.106.

7. G.R.S. Mead, p.173.

8. Origen, *An Exhortation To Martyrdom, Prayer and Selected Works*. Trans. and introd. by Rowan A. Greer. Preface by Hans Urs Von Balthasar. The Classics Of Western Spirituality, (New York, New York and Ramsey, New Jersey: Paulist Press 1979. © by The Missionary Society of St. Paul the Apostle in the State of New York), XXVII, pp.136-147.

9. Saint Basil the Great, in Nicene And Post-Nicene Fathers, second series, vol. VIII, trans. with notes by the Rev. Bloomfield Jackson M.A., (Grand Rapids, Michigan: Wm. B. Eerdmans Publishing Company, 1998 Repr.), *Prolegomena*, pp.lxi-lxii quoting from Homilies I and II on Fasting.

THE ANNUNCIATION

he Annunciation is recorded in the first chapter of the Gospel of Saint Luke (who was the first iconographer and who painted three icons of Mary from the life), in the *Protevangelium* of James (chapter 11) and the *Gospel of Pseudo-Matthew* (chapter 9). Both the *Protevangelium* and *Pseudo-Matthew* state that when the archangel Saint Gabriel first appeared to Mary, she was at a fountain about to fill a pitcher with water. This is the moment shown in our mosaic, and which Leonid Ouspensky and Vladimir Lossky say is of a rare type, known as the 'pre-Annunciation', only seen in icons depicting scenes from the life of Mary.[1] In our mosaic, Mary is shown at the well with a pitcher in her right hand, while her left arm, bent at the elbow, is raised, with flat palm, towards Saint Gabriel, who is hovering in the air, his right hand raised in salutation, his left holding his staff; the staff which is, accordingly (as an axial symbol) the sign of the messenger; in this case, the messenger of the Annunciation.

The well is circular in shape and sits on top of a step pyramid consisting of two platforms, and it has the same meaning as the bath which is being prepared in the mosaic of the Birth of Mary; and as with the bath and the vessel (represented here by the pitcher Mary is holding), so the well, the spring and the fountain are all Goddess symbols in that they all represent the womb of the Goddess as the source, in the form of the amniotic fluid of her womb, of the living, life-giving waters, the upper waters of Genesis, which are revelations of the Principle and Meaning of Mary.[2] The two platforms, forming a step pyramid, symbolise the mountain, also a symbol of the womb of the Goddess and, therefore, of Mary. We will discuss the mountain in greater detail in chapter 6.

The pitcher Mary is holding is the Holy Grail, the empty vessel and, as such, is a symbol of her meaning and, therefore, of the meaning of the Goddess and of our meaning too. It is for this reason that pottery was one of the three crafts (the other two being baking and weaving) which were practised in the temple of the Goddess during the Neolithic period and which were exclusively the preserve of women, because, in each case, the methodology of the craft and its end product were symbols of the womb of the Goddess as the source both of birth and of rebirth, as, indeed, is the temple itself; that is, they were symbols of the feminine principle and, therefore, of the Principle and Meaning of Mary and, accordingly, ultimately of the heart, which Mary is, as the dwelling-place of God's own perfect image of Himself.[3]

Pottery is made from clay, which is from the earth which, in its turn, as also stone and wood, is another symbol of Prime Matter and, accordingly, of the Principle and the Meaning of Mary, of which the pitcher is also a symbol. Having been born, as clay, of the Goddess (Mary), the pot is then returned to the womb of the Goddess, in the form of the kiln, to die and be reborn; for the pottery kiln, as the loom and the bread oven, is another symbol of the Principle and Meaning of Mary and, therefore, of the life-giving and regenerative womb of the Goddess.

The pitcher is golden. Because it does not tarnish and

also because of its radiance, gold symbolises the Divine Essence. It further represents the radiance of the transformed consciousness in the newly reborn soul. In both senses, this is the Goldenness of Aphrodite, The Golden One, of, that is, the Divine Love and Beauty, present in Its Totality and Wholeness in the heart of every person and which, by way of Self-Gift, is veiled in the forms of the world, but Whose Light, Whose Radiance, the Goldenness of Whose Beauty is witnessed in each and every instant by the Saints in the Unity in the multiplicity and in the multiplicity in the Unity.

Saint Gabriel is the messenger, the one who announces that God is the actuality both of ourselves and of the whole of creation. Saint Gabriel is said to have greeted Mary at the Annunciation with the Aramaic word *'Beshara'*. Aramaic was the language spoken by Mary and by Christ, and *'Beshara'* means 'Good news', 'Omen of Joy'. Here, in announcing to Mary that she is to be the mother of Jesus, Saint Gabriel is announcing to us that Mary is indeed the *Theotokos* and that it is by way of the combination of the Principle and Meaning of Mary and Grace that both Births take place within the soul; that is, he is announcing both the condition of our original creation and the means whereby we may return to that condition, which announcement is indeed *'Beshara'* for us.

When Saint Gabriel first appeared, Mary took refuge completely in God, but when she heard the *'Beshara'*, she submitted to the will of God with the complete submission which is her meaning, saying 'Behold the handmaid of the Lord; be it unto me according to thy word' (Luke 1. 38). What followed was the blowing-in of the Spirit into the place of pure, sheer, unconditioned and un-conditioning receptivity, which is the Meaning of Mary.

For the Second Birth to take place within us, we too must be the place of pure receptivity which Mary is and we must submit to the will of God with the complete submission which is the Meaning of Mary, which is the *'Potentia Obedientiaris'* of Saint Benedict. That is, we must be empty of ourselves, by dying to ourselves, so that, as in the Lord's Prayer, God's will ('Thy will') and not our will is done in us; or, as Bulent Rauf, said 'the beauty of free will is to give up free will for Him', so that, accordingly, God carries out His will in us as His own perfect 'image' and 'likeness'. In order to die to ourselves, to be empty of ourselves, we must say with Mary, and in the way that Mary said it: 'Behold the handmaid of the Lord; be it unto me according to thy word', regardless of our gender, for the words are from the heart, which is feminine, which, as the dwelling-place of the 'image' and the 'likeness' of God, is Mary. Perhaps one might even say that we should allow Mary herself to say the words for us and in us, since, by giving birth to Mary in our souls, we have, thereby, made Mary our mother too.

Because both the Annunciation and the Nativity are explicit demonstrations, not only of a physical birth, but also, and, perhaps, more importantly, of Spiritual birth (the two births) in Mary and Jesus (in His First Coming) only, spiritual virginity required its physical counterpart.

Thus, our mosaic is itself an announcement of the *'Beshara'* to us; the *'Beshara'* for us is that Mary does live in us and that she can be our mother too, and that if we allow her to say in us 'Behold the handmaid of the Lord; be it unto me according to thy word', then what follows for us is the birth of the soul back into God, which truly is *'Beshara'* for us.

Notes

[1] (a) *Protevangelium of James*, p. 363, *Pseudo-Matthew*, p.373. (b) For the Pre-Annunciation, see Leonid Ouspensky and Vladimir Lossky, *The Meaning of Icons*, p. 173, note 1.

[2] Marija Gimbutas, *Language of the Goddess*, p. 325 & Erich Neumann, *The Great Mother*, pp. 48 & 222.

[3] Marija Gimbutas, *Language of the Goddess* pp. 67-9, 147-50 (baking) & 238-9 (weaving) and Marija Gimbutas, *The Living Goddesses* Ed. and Supplemented by Miriam Robbins Dexter. [Marija Gimbutas died in 1994 before the book was finished] (Berkeley, Los Angeles & London: University of California Press, 1999), pp.72-4. See also Erich Neumann, *The Great Mother*, pp. 59-61, 121-4, 133-7 & 226-33.

THE NATIVITY

ary is shown lying on a bed before the cave in which, according to Tradition, Jesus was born. Jesus is lying in the manger, the crib, inside the cave. At the top of the mosaic, above the cave, is a hemisphere of light (the Divine realm) from which a shaft of light descends to the manger. To the right of Mary (our left) four angels are standing on the mountainside in prayer, whilst to the left of Mary (our right) another angel is announcing the birth of Jesus to three shepherds. Mary's gaze is fixed upon the bottom right hand corner of the mosaic, where two midwives are about to bathe Jesus, whilst in the bottom left hand corner, Saint Joseph is shown sitting, his head resting on his right hand, looking very gloomy indeed! In most icons of the Nativity, the positions of the bathing scene and Saint Joseph are reversed.

Saint Joseph's dejection is due to his doubts about, his inability to comprehend, the awesome mystery of the Virgin Birth, which, of itself, is an expression of our inability to comprehend. The look on Mary's face is of pure compassion, as shown in icons of the Virgin *Eleuosa* ('Our Lady of Compassion', the origin of which is one of the three icons of Mary painted from the life by Saint Luke); as in the Buddha of Unbearable Compassion; as also manifested in Tara, which Compassion is represented in China by the Goddess Kuan Yin (known as Kwan-non in Japan), all of whom are manifestations of the same Principle and Meaning.

Compassion here, that is, for Saint Joseph's—hence our—doubts and inability to comprehend, but which also encompasses the whole of creation and which prays and intercedes for the whole of creation. Because of which, Mary can look upon the horror of the crucifixion in full and complete knowledge (because she, and all the Saints, has and have 'the Mind of Christ') of the true spiritual meaning (the death to self, dying before we die) and she can look upon those who torture and abuse her son with Love and, thus, with Compassion and, accordingly, she can say, with Jesus, 'Father, forgive them; for they know not what they do' (Luke 23.34); for Mary and the Saints (by making Mary their mother too), are empty of themselves, which means that Mary and the Saints are filled to the full with God, thereby allowing Him to appear in them and to act in them as Himself in His own perfect 'image' and 'likeness'. Consequently, it is the Divine action, the Divine Love, which is *Agape*, the Divine Compassion which flows through Mary and the Saints; flows through her and them and out into the whole cosmos.

In all icons, whether of Jesus, Mary or the Saints, the gaze is both upon the divine 'image' and 'likeness' within themselves and, simultaneously, upon the Divine 'image' and 'likeness' within ourselves; ourselves, that is, as we truly are and not as we mistakenly believe ourselves to be. So, in that sense, it is a matter of God looking at Himself and at Himself in us as in His own perfect 'image'.

It is because Mary and the Saints are the dwelling-place of the 'image' and the 'likeness' of God, of the Love and the Beauty of God, that Mary, as the Blessed Virgin *Eleuosa*, Our Lady of Compassion and the Saints can pray both for ourselves and the whole of creation and say for us

'Father, forgive them....', to say, as Saint Isaac the Syrian (died c. 700) says:

> a man's heart burns for all creation—men, birds, animals, demons and all creatures. At their memory and sight his eyes shed tears. Great and powerful compassion fills a man's heart, and great suffering wrings it, so that he cannot endure, hear or see any harm or the least pain suffered by a creature. That is why he prays hourly, with tears, for dumb creation, for the enemies of truth, for those who harm him, that they should be preserved and shown mercy; he prays also for reptiles with a great compassion which wells up in his heart without measure until he becomes likened in this to God.[1]

Since God is the actuality both of ourselves and of the whole of creation and since we, as human becomings, are created according to the complete 'image' and 'likeness' of God, then we contain, by way of, and only by way of Self-Gift, the whole of creation within ourselves; then, in that sense, the sense in which Jesus says 'love thy neighbour as thyself' (Matthew 19. 19)—for our 'neighbour' is ourself—the whole of creation is also ourself; but, only by way of Self-Gift; for, then, when we are empty of ourselves, it is God loving Himself as Himself in us now as in His own perfect 'image' and 'likeness'.

Without any compulsion whatsoever, Mary is simply inviting us to enter our interiors, the secret cave of our hearts, which cave of the heart Mary is, wherein, and wherein alone, the meaning of the awesome mystery we are beholding resides and wherein, and wherein alone, it will be found.

The Tradition that the Nativity took place in a cave is recorded in both the *Protevangelium of James* and the *Gospel of Pseudo Matthew*.[2] The earliest extant mention of this

Tradition occurs in the *Dialogue with Trypho* of Saint Justin Martyr (c.100/110-165).[3] In one of his letters, Saint Jerome says that the cave of the Nativity was 'overshadowed' by the Grove of Tammuz, and in the cave where Jesus was born 'they used to mourn the beloved of Venus'.[4]

Tammuz, the beloved and the lover of the Semitic, Babylonian Goddess Ishtar, is a later name for Dumuzi, as Ishtar is a later name for Inanna. Later still, Inanna/Ishtar was to be called Aphrodite, and Dumuzi/Tammuz, Adonis (derived from the Semitic word '*Adon*', 'The Lord', 'The Master', which was the honorific title of Tammuz).

Dumuzi (alternating with his sister, Geshtinanna), Tammuz and Adonis each spent six months here with their beloved and six months in the underworld, symbolising death and rebirth, death and resurrection. Joseph Campbell says of Dumuzi (therefore also of Tammuz-Adonis) that he is 'the lord of the Tree of Life, the ever-dying, ever-resurrected Sumerian god who is the archetype of incarnate Being'.[5] Thus, Saint John taking Mary to Ephesus after the Crucifixion, represented a sealing by Mary of the principle of the Goddess, of which principle the Goddess in all her forms is a manifestation and Mary is the most sublime expression; so with the Nativity taking place in a cave associated with the 'ever-dying, ever-resurrected god who is the archetype of incarnate being', that principle was sealed in its most sublime expression by the Christ who is Jesus.

That principle is the Goddess and her son by Virgin Birth who is also her husband/lover, who dies and is resurrected.[6] The son who is the other who is no other. Other because, together with the moon (not least because of its phases, full, waning and waxing, its crescent and because it has no light of its own), the serpent (not least because it sheds its skin and hibernates) and the bull (not least because its horns, like the crescent moon, symbolise the empty vessel), he represents the sheer receptivity which results in the principle of death and rebirth, which is the affirmation that there is always and forever only Life, inherent in the cosmos as a whole (the new creation in each instant, for example), and in the sense of spiritual death and rebirth; of, that is, 'dying before we die'. The 'other', since the Goddess does not die to be reborn for she is eternal, immortal and indivisible and because he exists, as a becoming, only by way of Self-Gift; that is, he is, as Philo says, *'Theos'* but he is not *'O Theos'* (God, but not the God); who is no other for the Goddess is the creation to which she gives birth; that is, she is the actuality and, therefore the Truth both of her son and of the whole of her creation. The son, 'the lord of immortality', who is also her lover, for Love is the movement of creation.

In Christian mysticism, Mary is both the mother of Jesus and, as the soul, she is his Bride. The Bride, that is, of Christ, who is, as Jesus, her son and, as the Christ, her husband. Ultimately, that principle, by way of the Goddess mother by Virgin Birth (which principle in itself reaches its most sublime expression in Mary) is the principle of the two births; that is, of the two spiritual births.

The mountain and the cave were symbols of the Goddess, representing respectively her Holy Vulva (the cave) and her womb (the mountain) as the source both of birth and rebirth, of, that is, Virgin Birth, for the Goddess mother is the mother by Virgin Birth. Marija Gimbutas says that any mound, whether large or small, whether natural or artificial, including small artificial mounds such as loaves, symbolised the body and the womb of the Goddess. She has also pointed out that spending a night in a cave symbolised death and rebirth by returning via the Goddess's Holy Vulva to her womb to die and be reborn. The temple and the underground chamber, in that they also symbolised, originally, the cave and the mountain, served the same purpose. The remains of one such vulva-womb chamber can still be seen at the Asklepeion at Pergamon in Turkey. The sleeping in the cave, temple, underground chamber or tunnel was preceded by an ablution and fasting and was, she goes on to say, equated with 'slumbering in the goddess's uterus before spiritual reawakening. For the living, such a ritual brought physical healing and spiritual rebirth'.[7]

In his *Life of Moses*, Saint Gregory of Nyssa calls the mountain 'the mountain of the knowledge of God', in that it is far removed from the cares and worries of the world and, therefore, from the separate self. The mountain symbolises spiritual exaltation; that is, it represents the dwelling-place of God as He is both in Himself and, by way of Self-Gift, as He is in His own perfect 'image' and 'likeness'.[8]

Muhyiddin Ibn 'Arabi says that because stone has no movement of its own, in that it only moves when someone or something else moves it, it is, therefore, a symbol of the heart of the Saint, since, like stone, the heart of the Saint has no movement of its own, for the heart of the Saint is moved only by God. Hence, the hearts of the Saints conform themselves to the revelation of God, to the way in which God reveals Himself to them, which, in its turn, means that the Saints witness both the revelation and the One Who reveals Himself by way of that revelation; that is, they witness the unity in the multiplicity and the multiplicity in the unity. Whereas for us the opposite is the case, in that God reveals Himself to us in accordance with the way we are because by affirming and asserting ourselves, we determine over God by compelling Him to appear in us and to act in us as ourselves in us as His own perfect image only.

Thus, the cave is also the entrance into 'the mountain of the knowledge of God', which is God's Knowledge of Himself, the *Hagia Sophia*, the 'Mind of Christ' of Saint Paul, which one can equally well say is the Mind of the Buddha or, if one may use such an expression, the Mind of the *Tao*, and which is represented in Sumerian mythology by Enki and in Classical mythology by Athene. As it is also the entrance into the world axis, as also into the active, creative principle, as also into the womb of the Goddess, which is no other than the Principle and Meaning of Mary and without which entrance into the true 'mountain of the knowledge of God', the inner spiritual Mind, is impossible. Ultimately, as the Nativity demonstrates, the cave is a symbol of the heart as the dwelling-place of the 'image' of God, which cave, which heart, Mary herself is, and it is because of this that the Nativity took place in a cave. Thus, we are being shown both the condition of our original creation and the means, by realising and fulfilling within ourselves the Principle and the Meaning of Mary, thereby making Mary our mother too, whereby we may return to that condition.

In our mosaic here, and in all icons, the spiritual meaning is of far greater importance than the actual event itself. When a woman said to Jesus 'Blessed is the womb that bore thee, and the paps which thou hast sucked', Jesus replied, 'yea rather blessed are they that hear the word of God and keep it' (Luke 11. 27-8); of which saying Meister Eckhart says that the person who hears God's word and keeps it is more blessed than Mary was when she physically gave birth to Jesus. And such a person is more blessed in the sense that such a person, by making Mary her or his mother too, has given birth to Jesus spiritually in her or his soul; for again as Meister Eckhart says, God rejoices more in His birth into the Virgin soul (Mary), which is the birth of the soul back into God, than He rejoices in the physical birth of Jesus.[9]

This is the line of the Tradition established by Philo of Alexandria and continued by Saint Clement of Alexandria (c.150-215), Origen, Saint Gregory Thaumaturgos (c.213-270) and the four great Cappadocian Fathers, which was transmitted to the Cappadocians by Saint Macrina the Elder (died 340), the paternal grandmother of Saint

Macrina the Younger (died 379), Saint Basil the Great, Saint Gregory of Nyssa and Saint Peter of Sebaste (349-393) and who was herself taught either directly by Saint Gregory Thaumaturgos or by one of his pupils. This Tradition emphasised the spiritual rather than the literal meaning of the words of the Gospels, for as the Gospels themselves make plain, Christ took the disciples aside to explain the spiritual meaning of the parables.

Just as Mary is the physical mother of Jesus in this world, so is she the mother of His spiritual birth into the Virgin soul, the soul, that is, which is empty of the separate self, which soul Mary is; and only such a soul can truly keep the word of God, for then, if one may say such a thing, it is God keeping His own Word in Himself in us as in His own perfect 'image' and 'likeness'.

Unlike physical virginity which, once lost can never be regained, spiritual virginity can be regained; for the spiritual virginity which we possessed at our original creation and which we lose with the affirmation of ourselves, thereby becoming the woman taken in adultery of John 8. 3-11, is recovered by realising and fulfilling within ourselves the Principle and the Meaning of Mary, thereby making Mary our mother too. As Philo of Alexandria says: 'but when God begins to associate with the soul, He brings it to pass that she who was formerly woman becomes virgin again'.[10] This is why in icons of the Nativity, Mary is always shown outside the cave, sitting, as it were, in the mouth of the cave, in the entrance to it, for Mary, as has already been mentioned (in chapter 3) unites and combines within herself between the two spiritual births: that is, she is the sealing of the principle of spiritual virginity.

The manger, the crib, the cradle are manifestations of the empty vessel and, as such, they are the place of the soul newly reborn back into God, and which has, accordingly become as a child again, which must therefore grow up all over again and be re-educated, this time in the Divine

Wisdom. All of which proceeds from Origen's principle of belittling ourselves mentioned earlier (in chapter 4).

Once again we are being shown, in the Christ who is the child Jesus lying in the manger, that this is the meaning which lies hidden in the inner cave, the inner sanctum, of our hearts and that the supreme expression of that cave, of that sanctum of the heart, is the one who lies just at the entrance to the cave, Mary, and that by making Mary our mother too, the rebirth, which is the spiritual meaning of the birth we are witnessing, is possible for us.

In the figures of the shepherds, we have a universal spiritual symbol whose profound meaning has, as Richard Temple says, long been lost. For the ancient world, the shepherd was an image, on one level of its meaning, of the spiritual seeker; as anyone, he says, who has attempted any form of spiritual exercise realises immediately the difficulty of 'quietening the mind' and that, consequently, 'it is in this search for inner order that we find the analogy, widely employed in antiquity, of the shepherd'. All the inner distractions must be gathered together in one place, a place which is secure, from which they cannot escape and where they may be carefully watched and observed.[11] The sheepfold, the sheep-pen is the image of that place, as the shepherd is the image of the one who watches, symbolised, in Classical mythology by Hestia, the Goddess of the Hearth. The Hearth, at the centre of the house, the home; in the council chamber as the centre of the town, the city and at the centre of the state, the nation, the country, all of which are symbols of the heart. The shepherd, Hestia, facing inwards; the warrior Saint and/or the god of war facing outwards.

Thus, whenever anyone, irrespective of age, gender, background, nationality or creed, embarks upon a spiritual path, that person becomes, symbolically, a shepherd, just as, as Joseph Campbell says, that person also becomes a hero—or rather, becomes all the heroes of the entire world.

To ask whether Jason, Hercules, Gawain or Perceval or any other hero from all the myths from around the world ever existed as an historical personage is a profound misunderstanding of the purpose and meaning of myth and of the hero, for myth is parable, a revelation of profound spiritual principles and truths and its heroes, throughout all the myths of all the world, are archetypal manifestations of the spiritual seeker. Their purpose, as with the icon, is to point the way to, and chart the path of, the inner spiritual journey, the *Kenosis* of Christian spirituality, (of which principle, of which tradition, *The Story of O* by Pauline Réage is a sublime modern expression). Joseph Campbell says:

> Furthermore, we have not even to risk the adventure alone; for the heroes of all time have gone before us; the labyrinth is thoroughly known; we have only to follow the thread of the hero-path. And where we had thought to find an abomination, we shall find a god; where we had thought to slay another, we shall slay ourselves; where we had thought to travel outward, we shall come to the centre of our own existence; where we had thought to be alone, we shall be with all the world.[12]

At the highest level of its meaning, the shepherd is 'the inner guardian of the Mind', shepherding the pastures, the movements of the heart, keeping all in perfect rhythm, balance and harmony.[13] Saint John of Damascus (c.675-749/50) says that Saint Joachim 'habitually shepherded his inner thoughts in "Green Pastures"' (Psalm 23. 2).[14] The shepherd is thus, equally, the Saint and, at this level, is the Good Shepherd Who is the Christ, shepherding the pastures of the inner spiritual Mind. For, at this level, it is the one who can indeed say with Saint Paul, 'I live; yet not I, but Christ liveth in me' (Galatians 2. 20) and who can, therefore, say 'but we have the mind of Christ' (I Corinthians 2. 16), which is the same as saying 'I live, yet not I but the Buddha, or the *Tao*, lives in me' and 'but we have the Mind of the Buddha, or the *Tao*'. But, in order for this to be so for us, we must first make Mary our mother too.

The sheepfold-pen is, therefore, the place of both the spiritual seeker, as the place of spiritual training, and also and equally of the Saint, as the shepherd represents both the seeker and the Saint. So, here, the shepherds 'in the same country…abiding in the field, keeping watch over their flock by night' (Luke 2. 8), in that the shepherd is the inner guardian of the inner spiritual Mind, can refer equally to the seeker and the Saint.

Where one enters the church of Saint Saviour in Chora, two mosaics face one another. One is of the Virgin *Platytera*, known as 'Our Lady of the Sign', (*Platytera* means 'wider than, more spacious than') and which takes its name from Isaiah 7. 14, 'therefore the Lord himself shall give you a sign; Behold, a virgin shall conceive, and bear a son, and shall call his name Immanuel'. The mosaic belongs to the '*Orans*' (Prayer) group of icons in which Mary is shown with her arms uplifted in the ancient gesture of prayer, a gesture of receiving, which gesture is itself an expression of the Principle and Meaning of which Mary herself is the supreme expression. On her breast, that is, in her spiritual centre, is a roundel containing Christ Emmanuel (the Christ Child). The roundel is a Goddess symbol representing the Holy Vulva and Womb of the Goddess, again as symbols of the Principle and Meaning of Mary, by way of which Principle and Meaning and Grace the 'image' and the 'likeness' of God are born into the heart, the heart which Mary is. On the mosaic is written 'Mother of God. The Dwelling-Place of the Uncontainable', which paradox is resolved by the fact that the Uncontainable God is contained but only by Himself and by Himself in Mary, and, therefore in us when we have made Mary our mother too, as in His own perfect 'image' and 'likeness'.

Thus, as with icons of the Christ Child seated upon the lap of Mary, so here, we are looking at ourselves both as we are according to the condition of our original creation and as we are, or may be, if and when we return to that condition. As equally, we are looking at Heart of Mind, a demonstration, that is, of what it means to have 'the Mind of Christ'.

Facing this mosaic is a mosaic of Christ, upon which is written, 'Jesus Christ, The Land of the Living'. For so long as we affirm ourselves, we participate only partially in life because, by so doing, we determine over God by compelling Him to appear in us, to act in us and to live in us as ourselves in us as His own perfect image only. If however, we are empty of ourselves then we allow God to appear in us, to act in us and to live in us as Himself in us as His own perfect 'image' and 'likeness', and, accordingly, we participate in life to the full. It is by way of the Principle and Meaning of Mary, whose mosaic faces Christ, and Grace, that the lost 'likeness' is found and restored to the 'image' and then we too, by way of, and only by way of, Self-Gift, are the 'Dwelling-Place of the Uncontainable', for Mary, now our mother too, is that place in which the 'image' and the 'likeness' of the Uncontainable God dwells by way of Self-Gift, and, accordingly, we too live in 'the Land of the Living', for by way of Mary our mother and Grace, we are the land in which 'the Living' lives as in His own perfect 'image' and 'likeness'.

The same Greek word, 'Chora', appears on both mosaics, as 'Place' in the 'Dwelling-Place of the Uncontainable' and as 'Land' in 'the Land of the Living'. God is the 'place', the 'land' in which we live, for we live in God as our actuality, as Saint Luke says 'In God we live and move and have our being' (Acts 17. 28). Just as we live in God as our actuality, so God lives in us in that He manifests and reveals Himself in sensory forms by way of ourselves and the whole of creation. So, here, our shepherds 'in the same country', 'in the fields', are the possibility of ourselves as seekers becoming ourselves as Saints, as 'the Dwelling-Place of the Uncontainable' in 'the Land of the Living'.

On either side of these mosaics are mosaics depicting the wedding at Cana and the feeding of the five thousand. In the wine jars and the baskets (of loaves) once more we have symbols of Mary as the empty vessel, as in the bread and the wine we have the Eucharist, that is, the body (exterior) and the blood (spirit/interior) of Christ dwelling by way of Grace in Mary; and in us too, when we, as Origen says, through Grace, have made the Blessed Virgin our mother too, thereby enabling us to say with Saint Paul, 'I live; yet not I, but Christ liveth in me' (Galatians 2. 20).

In Sumerian mythology, before Inanna goes to visit Enki, the god of wisdom and water, in his abode, the Abzu (the 'Abyss', the 'Deep', the 'Sea'), she prepares herself spiritually, by placing the 'Shugurra, the crown of the steppe on her head' and then:

> She went to the sheepfold, to the shepherd. She leaned back against the apple tree. When she leaned against the apple tree, her vulva was wondrous to behold. Rejoicing at her wondrous vulva, the young woman Inanna applauded herself.[15]

In Sumerian, the same word means 'vulva', 'lap', 'loins', 'womb' and 'sheepfold', and the same pictographic sign originally stood for both vulva and sheepfold. The images are all familiar: the Holy Vulva and Womb of the Goddess as revelations of the Principle and Meaning of Mary as the source of both birth and rebirth; the tree as the world axis; and now the shepherd and sheepfold as well, all resulting in the fertility both of the whole cosmos and, particularly, spiritual fertility, Mind, that is, as Virgin and as Wife. The tree is an apple tree since the apple, both because of its roundness (symbol of totality, of wholeness) and because at its centre is a perfect vulva shape (the great womb of creation; that is, Prime Matter) and, therefore, of the Principle and Meaning of Mary.

Thus, as a symbol of the Principle and the Meaning of Mary, the sheepfold (as also the cattle byre, the cattle pen), represents both the means whereby that possibility (ourselves as seekers becoming ourselves as Saints) is realised and fulfilled within us and the resultant spiritual fertility of Mind as Virgin and as Wife.

It is also, as Philip Sherrard points out, the spiritual meaning of the injunction to be 'fruitful and multiply' (Genesis 1. 28), for in the Septuagint version of the Bible, the words which in the Authorised version are rendered thus, and which are, accordingly, interpreted as meaning (in the marriage ceremony) 'go forth and have many children', are translated into Greek as *'avxanesthe'* and *'plithinesthe'*, the former of which has the sense of 'grow' or 'become perfect' whilst the latter has the sense of 'make full' or 'increase'. Thus, he says, that whilst the Greek does have the sense in which it is understood according to convention, it could equally be read as 'grow to perfection and increase in spiritual fullness'.[16]

The opposite of this is that spiritual infertility in which, because we are alive to, or awake to, ourselves we are, accordingly, barren or sterile with regard to God, and which is demonstrated in the poetry of Enheduanna (born c. 2,300 BCE). Enheduanna, the daughter of king Sargon of Agade (c.2334-2279 BCE), was a high priestess of the god of the moon, Nanna, at Ur, but she was particularly devoted to Inanna. The first writer in history whose name is known, Enheduanna served as a model of excellence in all three of her roles of High Priestess, poetess and princess for centuries after her death. She writes of the sterility of such a state, when awareness of the indwelling of Inanna (Mary) and, therefore, of the divine, is not present:

> You have lifted your foot and left their barn of fertility. The women of the city no longer speak of love with their husbands. At night they do not make love. They are no longer naked before them, revealing intimate treasures.

Written in full knowledge of the meaning of both 'naked' (here, the soul stripped of the self, the *obex*), and 'making love' as symbols of the *Hieros Gamos*, the Sacred Marriage, as the union of the soul (which is feminine) with God, and of which Sacred Marriage, the relationship between two lovers is an outer manifestation; a principle which was widely known and understood throughout the ancient world. The 'city' in question is the heart.

Some seventeen hundred years later, on the island of her birth, Lesbos, another poetess sang in some sublime songs of the same Goddess, this time under her name Aphrodite. The songstress whom Socrates called 'the beautiful', who was known as the 'honey-tongued', whom Alcaeus, himself one of the great lyric poets of Greece, called the 'violet-haired, pure and honey-smiling', whom her contemporaries, and indeed many generations after, revered both as a poet and spiritual teacher, and to whom she was not only the greatest of the nine great lyric poets of Greece, but was, as Plato called her, 'the Tenth Muse': Sappho; Sappho, 'violet-haired, pure, honey-smiling, Sappho'. Enheduanna and Sappho, priestess, poetesses, singers, whose lives were devoted to the service of, and whose songs were celebrations of, the Goddess of Love and Beauty; that is, whose lives were devoted to the service of, and whose songs were celebrations of, the Divine Love and Beauty, the Love and Beauty of God.[17]

This is how the injunction of Christ and Saint Paul to 'pray without ceasing' (I Thessalonians 5. 17) is fulfilled within us, since, when we are empty of ourselves, we allow God to appear, to live and to act in us as Himself in us as His own perfect 'image' and 'likeness', and, accordingly, as Meister Eckhart says, now 'God performs His own work...and God is His own place of work, being a worker in Himself', as, now, 'the soul neither knows, nor works, nor loves, anymore, but God through the soul knows and works and loves'.[18]

Dom Sylvester often referred to the saying of Saint Basil the Great who, when asked by a monk how the Apostles had time for prayer with all the duties they had to perform, replied that the Apostles made prayer what they did, therefore, everything the Apostles did was prayer, because the Apostles were empty of themselves, and, accordingly, God was acting as Himself in them as in His own perfect 'image' and 'likeness'. This is so, as Dom Sylvester never tired of saying, 'wherever we are and whatever we may be doing, even when we are doing the shopping and the washing-up', because, he said, what constitutes constant prayer is the constant awareness at Heart of Mind of our own nothingness, that we exist, that is, as becomings not as beings, as becomings actualised by Self-Gift and whose actuality God is. If and when we are constantly aware of this by having the barrier of self, which we create through our resentment of becoming, removed from us by way of the combination of the Principle and Meaning of Mary and Grace, then we are, accordingly, constantly aware of the presence of God 'whether we are doing the shopping or the washing-up', and which he called (with reference to the *Qur'anic* verse mentioned below) 'the spirituality of the market place'.

Then, as Dom Sylvester said, we are truly the *Domus Dei*, the *Baytu-llâh*, the House and the Household of God, in which God carries out His chores. Saint Basil the Great says, 'it is the part of a really great man not only to be sufficient for great things, but by his influence to make small things great'.[19] Which is the same as the saying of Christ: 'He that is faithful in that which is least is faithful also in much: and he that is unjust in the least is unjust also in much' (Luke 16. 10).

These are the people of whom the Holy *Qur'an* says that even in the midst of buying and selling in the market place they are not distracted even for an instant from the rememoration of God. As Saint Gregory Nazianzos says, for such people, because they are empty of themselves, it is no longer a matter of them praying to God, but rather of God 'offering prayer or adoration to Himself'.[20] This is the twelfth degree of Humility of Saint Benedict in which 'work is done without effort and as if naturally'.[21] Which prayer is, as Evagrios of Pontos says, 'the converse of Mind', of Heart of Mind, 'with God', which is God's converse with Himself in us as His own perfect 'image' and 'likeness'.[22] Our mosaic is showing us that this is possible for us too, and that Mary, the Principle and Meaning of Mary, is an essential factor in attaining that condition.

As the 'inner guardian' of the spiritual Mind, the shepherd is closely related to Enki and, therefore, to spiritual fertility, to Mind as Virgin and as Wife, and, accordingly, in our mosaic, to Christ, which is why Inanna begins her preparations by going to 'the shepherd and the sheepfold'. Inanna receives from Enki the Holy *Me*, the sacred laws of the universe. The Holy *Me* were, for the Sumerians, what *Maat* was for the ancient Egyptians, what *Dharma* is in India, the *Tao* in the far east, and Truth in Christian spirituality, which, as Joseph Campbell says,

> Refers to the law, truth, or order of the universe, which is the law, truth, order, and way of each being and thing within it, according to its kind... this Chinese conception of the one beyond names,

which, becoming two, produced of itself the ten
thousand things and is therefore within each as
the law—the *Tao*, the way, the sense, the order and
substance of its being.[23]

Because God is His Knowledge of Himself, because
He is His own Word, in knowing Himself as He Himself
is, God knows each *logos* hidden within the *Logos* and, in
knowing Himself God knows Himself as the Truth, that is,
as the actuality, and, therefore, as the Truth of each *logos*.
And the Truth of each *logos*, of, that is, both ourselves and
the whole of creation, is God as our actuality.

Self-Gift is God's Self-Gift of Himself to Himself as He
Himself is, which Gift is received by each *logos* individuated
in that movement, each according to its capacity to receive,
which capacity is determined by what it itself is, but God
gives the whole of Himself, whole and entire; and this is
what is meant by Truth, in Christian spirituality, by the *Tao*,
by *Dharma*, by *Maat* and by the Holy *Me*.

In his 'Ode on a Grecian Urn', John Keats wrote,
'Beauty is truth, truth Beauty, that is all Ye know on earth,
and all ye need to know'. God's Self-Gift of Himself to
Himself is the Gift of Himself to Himself as Beauty, sheer,
absolute Beauty, and Bulent Rauf said that the movement
of Self-Gift, the movement in which Self-Gift takes place,
is Love: 'Love', he said, 'is the movement of Beauty'. Our
mosaic is showing us that this very Beauty, by way, and
only by way of Self-Gift, dwells within the heart of each
and every person, and if we truly knew the meaning of
what is being shown to us, of the words of the poet, then
those words would indeed be fulfilled within us. This is
also the meaning of Truth, the *Tao*, *Dharma*, *Maat* and the
Holy *Me*. And this is why it is Inanna (as no other than
Mary), as the Goddess of the Divine Love and Beauty, of
the Love and Beauty of God, who receives the Holy *Me*,
as, supremely, Mary in the movement of Self-Gift, which

is Love, gives birth to the 'image' and the 'likeness' of Beauty in the heart, which Mary is, as by way of Mary, in the movement which is Love, the soul is born back into Beauty as the lost 'likeness' is restored to the 'image'. Born back, that is, into God, and, therefore, into Beauty, its source and its actuality and which it never, save in an illusory thought, left.

Philo of Alexandria says, with reference to the heart, that its Sole Inhabitant is God, for God is 'the *Monos Politès*', and God is the '*Monos Politès*' because God is the actuality both of ourselves and of the whole of creation.[24] It is for this reason, because they perceive that God is 'the *Monos Politès*', that, as Saint Basil the Great says, the Saints, 'even in a crowd, are always alone with themselves and with God', wherever they are and whatever they may be doing.[25]

In his *Treatise On Virginity*, Saint Gregory of Nyssa says, as has already been mentioned, that because the Nativity is a demonstration not so much of a physical birth (though it is indeed also that) but of spiritual birth, of, that is, the birth both of God into the soul and of the soul back into God, that Jesus 'did not come into the world by wedlock' (which is also why, in his First Coming which is the spiritual First Birth, Jesus did not marry). He goes on to say that when we are empty of ourselves (which is the spiritual virginity, which Saint Gregory calls 'the virgin life' in the following quote), when we have given birth to Mary in our souls, thereby making Mary our mother too, that:

> What happened in the stainless Mary when the fullness of the Godhead which was in Christ shone out through her, happens in every soul which leads by rule the virgin life. No longer indeed does the Master come with bodily presence…but spiritually, He dwells in us and brings His Father with Him.[26]

Saint Gregory says that it is indeed possible for each and every one of us 'to be the mother of such a son; as our Lord says 'He that doeth my will is my brother, my sister, and my mother' (Matthew 12. 50).[27] This is indeed what our mosaic is showing to us 'silently and by way of representation'.

Notes

[1] Quoted by Leonid Ouspensky and Vladimir Lossky in *The Meaning Of Icons*, pp.92-93 with reference, note 2, page 93 to V.N. Lazarev, *The Art of Novgorod* (Moscow-Leningrad, 1947), p.114, quoting from *Ascetic Discourses of our Holy Father Isaac of Syria*, (Moscow, 1858).

[2] *Protevangelium of James*, chapter 18, p.365. *Pseudo-Matthew*, chapter 13, p.374.

[3] Saint Justin Martyr, *Dialogue with Trypho*, is included in Ante-Nicene Fathers, vol. 1, The Apostolic Fathers, with Justin Martyr and Irenaeus. American Edition, Chronologically Arranged, with Brief Notes and Prefaces by A. Cleveland Cox D.D., (Edinburgh: T&T Clark and Grand Rapids, Michigan: Wm. B. Eerdmans Publishing Company, 1989 repr.), chapter 78, p.237.

[4] For Saint Jerome's letter, Jerome to Paulinus: see *Protevangelium of James*, chapter 18, footnote 4, p. 365.

[5] Joseph Campbell, *The Masks of God*, vol. III, Occidental Mythology, p.14.

[6] For the Principle of the Goddess mother by Virgin Birth and her lover-son, see *The Masks of God*, vol. II Oriental Mythology, pp. 39-40.

[7] Marija Gimbutas, *The Language of the Goddess*, for the mountain as womb, pp. 148-9; for loaves, pp. 147-9; for sleeping in a cave, pp. 151-9, particularly 158, see also *The Living Goddesses*, p.62.

8 Saint Gregory of Nyssa, *Life of Moses*, no.152, p.91.

9 Meister Eckhart M. O'C Walsh edition, Sermon 89, p.285 and Sermon 53, p. 61.

10 Philo of Alexandria in G.R.S. Mead, p.151.

11 Richard Temple, *Icons And The Mystical Origins Of Christianity*, pp.6-7.

12 Joseph Campbell, *The Hero With A Thousand Faces*, (London: Paladin, 1988), p.25.

13 Richard Temple, *Icons And The Mystical Origins Of Christianity*, pp. 6-7.

14 Saint John of Damascus, *On The Dormition Of The Holy Mother Of God, Homily 1*, included in On The Dormition Of Mary: Early Patristic Homilies. Trans. and Introd. by Brian E. Daley, S.J., (Crestwood, New York: St. Vladimir's Seminary Press, 1998), p. 189.

15 Diane Wolkstein and Samuel Noah Kramer, *Inanna Queen of Heaven and Earth*, p.12.

16 Philip Sherrard, *The Sacred In Life And Art* (Ipswich: Golgonooza Press, 1990), pp. 121-122.

17 For Enheduanna see William W. Hallo and J. J. A. Van Dijk, *The Exaltation of Inanna* (New Haven and London: Yale University Press, 1968), pp.1-11 (role of excellence, p.1). See also Aliki and Willis Barnstone, Editors, *A Book of Women Poets from Antiquity to Now* (New York: Schocken Books, 1980), p.1. The quote is from p.4, but was 'adapted by Aliki and Willis Barnstone' from William W. Hallo and J.J.A. Van Dijk *The Exaltation of Inanna* and appears on lines 54-57 of the Exaltation, pp.20 (transliteration of the original) and 21 (translation). See also Nancy Qualls Corbett, *The Sacred Prostitute: Eternal Aspect of the Feminine* (Toronto: Inner City Books, 1988), pp.26-30. For Sappho see Paul Friedrich, *The Meaning of Aphrodite*, (Chicago and London: The University of Chicago Press, 1978), pp.108-110, 113, 117, 123-128.

[18] Meister Eckhart, M. O'C. Walsh edition, Sermon 87, p. 274.

[19] Saint Basil the Great, Nicene And Post-Nicene Fathers, second series, volume VIII, Letter 98, p. 182.

[20] Saint Gregory Nazianzos, *The Fifth Theological Oration: On The Holy Spirit*, included in Nicene Fathers, p. 321.

[21] Saint Benedict, *The Rule Of Saint Benedict In English* Ed. Timothy Fry O.S.B., (Collegeville, Minnesota: The Liturgical Press, 1982), p. 38.

[22] Evagrios The Solitary, 'On Prayer' 3, *The Philokalia*, vol. 1, p. 57

[23] Joseph Campbell, *The Masks of God*, vol. II, Oriental Mythology, pp. 23 & 25.

[24] René Guénon, *Fundamental Symbols*, p.309, note 8, but without reference to the source in Philo.

[25] *The Philokalia*, vol. III, Saint Basil quoted by Saint Peter of Damaskos, p.155.

[26] Saint Gregory of Nyssa, *On Virginity*, included in Nicene And Post-Nicene Fathers, vol. V, Saint Gregory Of Nyssa. Trans. with Prolegomena, Notes And Indices by William Moore and Henry Austin Wilson, (Grand Rapids, Michigan: Wm. B. Eerdmans Publishing Company, 1979 repr.), chapter II, pp. 344-345.

[27] ibid. chapter XIII. pp. 359-60.

THE CRUCIFIXION

he mosaic of the Crucifixion no longer exists, but it is generally believed to have been in the nave. In his exposition on the meaning of the cross, Saint Gregory of Nyssa says that there are four arms, four projections, which emerge from and converge upon a central point, giving length, breadth, depth and height, all the directions, all the dimensions of space, symbolising thereby the presence of God as actuality everywhere and in all things.[1] The central point representing the divine essence, the Principial Unity, wherein all the *logoi* are hidden in a state of non-individuation, as colours, say, in light, or as sounds in the breath, wherein all the contraries are resolved and transcended and from which they emerge, as no other. Thus, in the emerging from and the converging upon, we have the two movements, the two currents of manifestation and the third which unites and combines within itself between the two, as well as, with regard to us, the two births. Accordingly, it symbolises the vision of the Saint, who perceives the unity (as actuality) in the multiplicity, by means of which God manifests and reveals Himself in sensory forms, and the multiplicity in the unity (as actuality). This, the resolution of the contraries, is another of the meanings demonstrated in Agnolo Bronzino's masterpiece *Allegory of Love (Venus With Cupid, An Allegory)*.

Thus, the cross shows forth 'silently and by way of representation' the meaning of Christ's words 'I am the vine and ye are the branches' (John 15.5), as it shows forth the meaning of the words of Saint Paul 'God is all, in all' (Colossians 3.11) and the meaning of the words of Saint Luke 'in God we live and move and have our being' (Acts 17.28). Accordingly, the cross is both a symbol of the whole of creation and of ourselves, both according to the condition of our original creation and as we may be if, and when, we return to that condition. In this sense, it is the same as the mirror in Velázquez's painting *The Rokeby Venus (The Toilet Of Venus)* in which Aphrodite is looking at herself in the mirror of herself as her own perfect 'image' and 'likeness'.

The spiritual death, the death to self, the dying before we die of the Prophet Mohammad, is the spiritual meaning of the Crucifixion. As was mentioned in chapter 2 (The Birth of Mary), the veil which covered the entrance to the Holy of Holies in the temple was rent asunder at the time of the Crucifixion (Matthew 28.51, Mark 15.38, Luke 23.45). This veil, in its turn, symbolises the veil of self which, by affirming ourselves, we place between ourselves and God as He Himself is and which veil, the *obex* of Saint Benedict, is rent asunder at the time of our crucifixion: that is, when we are crucified to ourselves, when we die before we die, thereby permitting us to enter the true Holy of Holies of our hearts, wherein dwells God's own perfect 'image' of Himself as He Himself is, and which is, accordingly, the 'Dwelling-Place of the Uncontainable', which Mary is. It is also the veil with which God veils Himself (as in Sandro Botticelli's *The Birth of Venus*) which veil is equally rent asunder at the time of our crucifixion, for, in dying to ourselves we have, as Meister Eckhart urges us to do, seized God in His wardrobe.

This, the birth of the soul back into God, is, as Origen says, the spiritual meaning of the Second Coming of Christ. However, for this to be so for us we must first make Mary our mother too, as Christ Himself says:

> Then one said unto him, Behold, thy mother and thy
> brethren stand without, desiring to speak with thee.
> But he answered and said unto him that told him,
> Who is my mother? And who are my brethren?
> And he stretched forth his hand toward his disciples,
> and said, Behold my mother and my brethren!
> For whosoever shall do the will of my Father
> which is in Heaven, the same is my brother, and
> sister, and mother.
> (Matthew 12. 47-50)

And, on the cross:

> When Jesus therefore saw his mother, and the
> disciple standing by, whom he loved [Saint John]
> he saith unto his mother, Woman behold thy son!
> Then saith he to the disciple, Behold thy mother!
> And from that hour that disciple took her unto his
> own home.
> (John 19. 26-7).

Origen says, with reference to Christ's words from
the cross:

> No one can apprehend the meaning of it except he
> have lain on Jesus's breast and received from Jesus
> Mary to be his mother also. Such an one must he
> become who is to be another John, and to have
> shown to him, like John, by Jesus Himself, Jesus
> as He is. For if Mary, as those who declare who
> with sound Mind extol her, had no other son but
> Jesus, and yet Jesus says, to His mother, 'Woman,
> behold thy son', and not 'behold you have this
> son also', then He virtually said to her 'Lo, this is

Jesus, whom thou didst bear'. Is it not the case that
everyone who is perfect lives himself no longer, but
Christ lives in him; and if Christ lives in him, then
it is said of him to Mary, 'Behold thy son Christ'.[2]

Thus, Origen says that everyone who does the will
of the Father in Heaven is Christ's mother[3] and Meister
Eckhart says the same: 'The Father speaks the Word into
the soul, and when the 'son' is born every soul becomes
Mary'.[4] For this to be so for us too, like Saint John, 'from
that hour' we must take Mary into our home too (here,
'home' symbolises the heart), so that we may give birth to
Mary in our souls, thereby, making Mary our mother too,
and it is then, and only then, that we can say with Saint
Paul 'I live; yet not I, but Christ liveth in me' (Galatians 2,
20), and it is thus that Mary is indeed both the *Theotokos*
and the *Hodigitria* (the One Who Shows the Way).

It is, perhaps, in this sense and with this meaning, that
the Christ who is Jesus addresses Mary as 'woman' both
here and at the Wedding at Cana (John 2. 4, the meaning of
which is also spiritual death and rebirth); Mary is 'Woman',
the embodiment of the Divine Feminine; of, that is, sheer
receptivity, by way of which, together with Grace, God is
born into the soul and the soul is born back into God.

That everyone who does the will of the Father in
Heaven is not only the mother of Christ, but also both his
'sister' and 'brother' as well is the sealing of a very ancient
principle, which we have already come across in the Virgin
Goddess Mother, who is Mary, and her son lover, who
dies and is resurrected and which is symbolised by Inanna
and Dumuzi, Ishtar and Tammuz, Cybele and Attis and
Aphrodite and Adonis.

In Sumerian mythology, after her symbolic resurrection
and return from 'the Great Below', Inanna banishes Dumuzi
to the underworld,[5] demonstrating thereby, the need for
us to sacrifice the 'father', 'husband' 'son'; the 'husband'

who 'is not thy husband' of the woman of Samaria (John 4. 18), which is the same as the injunction in Psalm 45. 10-11, 'Daughter leave thy father's house and the king will greatly desire thy beauty'. The house we must leave, as Dom Sylvester never tired of saying, is the house of the 'father' who is not our 'Father', of the 'husband' who is not our 'Husband', which is the separate self, in order that we may die and be reborn in the Resurrection which is the restoration of the lost 'likeness' to the 'image', so that we may, thereby, dwell in the House of the 'Father' Who truly is our 'Father', the House, that is, of 'Our Father Who art in Heaven', which is the *Domus Dei*, the *Baytu-llâh*, in which, as Dom Sylvester says, 'God carries out His chores'. Which is the House in which we truly dwell did we but know it.

Geshtinanna offers to take his place, and the six-monthly alternation is decreed by Inanna, which is the sacrifice of the self, so beautifully demonstrated by Inanna herself in her descent.[6] Wandering about the city (the heart) Geshtinanna (Mary), looking for her brother, mourning for her brother; which yearning is the yearning which is *Eros*; which is the mourning of the Beatitude, and which, as Beatitude Itself promises, will be comforted. Geshtinanna says: 'O my brother! Who is your sister? I am your sister. O Dumuzi! Who is your mother? I am your mother'.[7]

By way of the Principle and Meaning of Mary/ Geshtinanna, Dumuzi experiences spiritual death and rebirth because he has made Geshtinanna (Mary) his mother too. Ultimately, the principle is of the resurrection of the soul through death and rebirth in the womb of the Virgin Goddess Mother who is Mary. Which means that God is our Father in the sense that He is the Father of the Christ Who is Jesus; not, as formerly, the Father of ourselves in us as His own perfect image only, but now of Himself, as He Himself is, in us as His own perfect 'image' and 'likeness', which, in its turn, means that we are not only the mother of Christ (since we have now made Mary our mother too), but both his sister and his brother also because we are now truly of the family of Christ (for we can now indeed say, with Saint Paul, 'I live; yet not I, but Christ liveth in me'); thus, we contain the sister and the brother within ourselves. Therefore, we are Christ's mother, sister and brother as we are, equally, none: for we have that within us wherein the opposites (sister and brother) are resolved and transcended, as colours in light or sounds in the breath. However, this is by way of, and only by way of, Self-Gift, and because, and only because, we have taken Mary to live with us in our homes, thereby giving birth to Mary in our souls, thereby making Mary our mother too.

One of the consequences of this is that we obtain peace, the peace which Christ gives and of which He says, 'peace I leave with you, my peace I give unto you: not as the world giveth, give I unto you' (John 14. 27).

'Not as the world giveth', because this is the peace which is Salaam, the peace of, and which is, perfection. Peace is the absence of discord, and when one witnesses the unity, as source and actuality, in the multiplicity and the multiplicity in the unity, as source and actuality, then there is no discord, and, therefore, there is peace, for then we witness, as Joseph Campbell says, 'that there is the peace of eternal being within every aspect of the field of temporal becoming'.[8]

Further, when we have been crucified to ourselves, then, as Christ says, we are no longer the servants of God, but His friends:

> Henceforth I call you not servants: for the servant knoweth not what his lord doeth: but I have called you friends; for all things that I have heard of my Father I have made known unto you. (John 15. 15)

Thus, as God's own perfect 'image' and 'likeness' of Himself, as no longer His servant, but His friend, we enter into *Parresia*, complete and total intimacy with God, which is the *Uns* of Islam; because, and only because, God has declared us, now that we are empty of ourselves, worthy of being called His friend, as in the Odyssey when, after having been led through the process of spiritual death and rebirth and having been instructed in the Divine Wisdom by Aphrodite, Athene and Hermes via Circe, Calypso and Nausicaa, Nausicaa can declare that Odysseus is now worthy of being her husband. Saint Gregory of Nyssa says of this friendship:

> This is true perfection: not to avoid a wicked life because like slaves we servilely fear punishment, nor to do good because we hope for rewards, as if cashing in on the virtuous life by some business-like contractual arrangement. On the contrary, disregarding all those things for which we hope and which have been reserved by promise, we regard falling from God's friendship as the only thing dreadful and we consider becoming God's friend the only thing worthy of honor and desire. This, as I have said, is the perfection of life.[9]

This is why, according to tact (*Adab*, in Arabic), in the tact of the language of Love, in the tact of the language of the intimacy of Love, which is the Intimacy between God as sheer absolute Beauty and Himself, as sheer absolute Beauty, in His own perfect 'image' and 'likeness' (Aphrodite looking at herself in the mirror in Velázquez's painting), we refer to God as 'He'. Yes, God is indeed both He and She (the word for Essence in Arabic, *Dhât*, is feminine, with the sense of 'womb'), as He is equally indeed neither, but, here, 'He' refers not to gender but to the active creative principle. In Islamic mysticism it is said that 'we are *haqq*, but we are not

Al Haqq.' Haqq is one of the Most Beautiful Names of God and means the True, the Real. This is the same as the saying of Philo of Alexandria, that 'we are *Theos,* but we are not *O Theos'*, 'we are God, but we are not The God'[10] which is the same as the 'adoption' (what the Word is by nature, we are by way of 'adoption') of Christian spirituality; all of which sayings are acknowledging and affirming that we exist by way of, and only by way of, Self-Gift. So, by referring to God as 'He' we are acknowledging and affirming, in the tact of the language of Love, Beauty, and Intimacy that 'we are *haqq,* but we are not *Al Haqq'*, that 'we are *Theos,* but we are not *O Theos'*, that what the Word is by nature, we are only by way of 'adoption'.

This is what our mosaic is showing us 'silently and by way of representation', that it is indeed possible for Christ to say to Mary of us 'Behold thy son', but for this to be indeed so for us He must first say to us of Mary, 'Behold thy mother'.

Notes

[1] Saint Gregory of Nyssa, Nicene Fathers, *The Great Catechism,* chapter XXX1, p. 500.

[2] Origen, *Commentary On John,* Ante-Nicene Fathers, Book 1, chapter 6, p.300.

[3] ibid. Book 2, chapter 6, p. 330.

[4] Quoted by R.A. Nicholson in *Rumi, Poet And Mystic* (London: Mandala Books, Unwin Paperbacks, 1978), p. 121, footnote 3, with reference to Inge, *Christian Mysticism,* p.162 seq.

[5] Diane Wolkstein and Samuel Noah Kramer, *Inanna,* p. 71.

[6] ibid, pp. 88-9.

[7] ibid. p. 87.

[8] Joseph Campbell, *The Masks of God,* volume II, Oriental Mythology, p. 82.

[9] Saint Gregory of Nyssa, *Life Of Moses,* p. 137.

[10] Quoted in G.R.S. Mead, p. 160.

THE KOIMESIS, THE DORMITION, THE ASSUMPTION OF MARY

he feast of the *Koimesis*, the Dormition of Mary, known in the west as the Assumption of Mary, is celebrated on 15 August. In our mosaic, Mary is shown on her bed, standing beside which is Christ in Glory, surrounded by a double Mandorla containing angels, at the apex of which is one of the Seraphim. Christ is holding the soul of Mary, which is depicted as a child wrapped in white. Around the bed are the Apostles, Saint James the Less (the brother of Jesus, and first bishop of Jerusalem, who was martyred c.63) and three disciples of the Apostles: Saints Timothy, Hierotheos and Dionysios the Areopagite (originally thought to have been, but now known not to have been, the Saint Dionysios the Areopagite referred to earlier, which Saint Dionysios is now believed to have flourished sometime between 476 and 533). The chamber is being incensed.

The Mandorla (from the Italian for almond, because of its shape) which always surrounds Christ in Glory, is itself, originally, a Goddess symbol which represented the Holy Vulva and Womb of the Goddess and is, accordingly, a symbol of Mary. The meaning here is of Christ (the same is equally true of the Saint) containing within Himself not only the divine essence but also all the realms of becoming, from the very highest to the very lowest, as in the descent of Inanna from 'The Great Above' to the 'The Great Below' and all that lies in between 'The Great Above' and 'The Great Below'.

The incense is itself a symbol of the soul in which the Second Birth has taken place, for then, as Saint Paul says, we live, yet no longer us but Christ (or the Buddha or the *Tao*) lives in us. Then, because God lives in us as Himself in us as His own perfect 'image' and 'likeness' we too, with Saint Paul, are 'unto God a sweet Savour of Christ' (II Corinthians 11. 15).

Christ is holding the soul of Mary in the form of a child. Some of the meanings inherent within the image of the child were discussed in chapter 4 (the mosaic of the Presentation of Mary into the Temple), so, suffice it to say here that because the child is symbolically closer to its source, to the origin, to the essence, it represents both the First and the Second Births, which are the First and the Second Comings of Christ, the Second in the sense that Origen gives of 'belittling ourselves'. With regard to us, the child is, therefore, another symbol of the Principle and Meaning of Mary. Just as Christ Emmanuel (as in the mosaic of the Virgin *Platytera* already mentioned) represents the eternal pre-existent *Logos*, the Word Who is also the Image, so here, this child represents the soul of Mary, which is the essence of the Principle and Meaning of Mary, which is the Feminine Principle and who is, therefore, both the '*Theotokos*' and the '*Hodigitria*', returning to the source she has never left, as Saint John of Damascus says:

> Today she receives the beginning of a new existence from the one who gave her the beginning of her former existence—she who gave the beginning of a second existence, in a body, to him who had no temporal beginning to his previous eternal existence, even though he has the Father as the beginning and cause of his own divine being.[1]

and:

> He, who came down from his super-essential
> immaterial height, beyond all things, without ever
> leaving the Father's heart…and raised to the land
> of heaven the one who is called 'heaven on earth'.[2]

Just as, in Eternity, this principle is born of the Father, through the Word in the Spirit in the movement of Self-Gift, the movement which is Love, so, in Eternity, by way of this Principle, from the Father, in the Spirit, is the Word, Who is also the 'image', born into the soul as 'image', the soul which the Principle and Meaning of Mary is. Just as by way of this Principle, in the Spirit, through the Word is the soul born back into the Father. For, as Saint John of Damascus says, Mary 'is the bridal chamber of the Word's holy incarnation'.[3]

Our mosaic is showing us that the Principle and Meaning of Mary, the principle which is the eternal feminine, which is the principle of complete submission to God, to Buddha-hood, to the *Tao*, is eternal and universal, that it is for all people, in all places and for all times; and that it is by way of the Principle and Meaning of Mary that it is possible for us, by making Mary our mother too, to be, what we already are, did we but know it: 'the bridal chamber of the Word's holy incarnation'.

Notes

[1] Saint John of Damascus included in *On The Dormition of Mary*, Brian F. Daley S.J., Homily III, On The Dormition of Our Lady, The Mother of God, 4, p. 235.

[2] ibid. 1, p. 232.

[3] ibid. 2, p. 233.

CONCLUSION

s was mentioned in the Introduction, the Orthodox Churches afford the icon equal status with the Gospels because they come from the same source; that is, like the Gospels, the Holy *Qur'an*, the Torah and all the sacred books of all Traditions, like all the writings of all the Saints, the source is revelation. Therefore, for a representation to be an icon it must not be according to the conception of the individual who paints it. As the Apostles 'made prayer what they did' because they were not there, therefore God was appearing and acting in them as Himself in His own perfect 'image' and 'likeness', so the iconographer must, by making Mary his mother too, be empty of himself, so that he is thereby able to realise and fulfil within himself the principles and meanings of which the icon is a revelation. He must, that is, be in a place of such pure receptivity, which place Mary is, that he is able to receive the icon, and, therefore, the principles and meanings it reveals, as it, and they, are given to him.

All icons have but one purpose, which is to show to us both the condition of our original creation as according to the 'image' and the 'likeness' of God and the means whereby we may return to that condition. That is, their purpose is to point us to our own interiors wherein, and wherein alone, the meaning lies, and wherein and wherein alone, it will be found. The same is true of all sacred art in whatever medium: architecture, sculpture, painting, drama, literature—as, for example, Classical Greek drama and the works of William Shakespeare. An essential prerequisite for rediscovering the lost 'likeness' so that it may be restored to the 'image' is the Principle and Meaning of Mary. By way of this Principle and Meaning it is possible for us too to be the 'Dwelling-Place of The Uncontainable', 'the bridal chamber of the Word's holy incarnation' in the 'Land of the Living', by way of the one who is 'heaven on earth' to be 'heaven on earth'.